The Essence of the Bhagavad Gita

© – 1st German edition 2015
Original title: "Die Essenz der Bhagavad-Gita"
© – 1st Englisch edition 2015
Dr. Bernd Helge Fritsch
www.berndhelgefritsch.com
Email: office@berndhelgefritsch.com

English translation: Peter Hessel,
Delmenhorst, Germany, www.peterhesseltranslator.com

Design & Layout: Dr. Evelyn Schmelzer

Graphic in the book: Karin Wimmer

Produced and published by
BoD - Books on Demand,
Norderstedt
ISBN 9783738626278

The book

This book results from the author's decades of in-depth studies of Eastern spirituality.

The Bhagavad Gita combines the most beautiful pearls of Ancient Indian wisdom into a wonderful entity. The "Song of the Sublime" thoroughly explains all the important subjects of the earthly and the divine world.

The Gita provides us with one of the most valuable and beautiful revelations mankind has ever received. Its verses open a gate to spiritual self-recognition and to a discovery of the divine.

This edition of the Gita offers today's readers a most practical access to its essence thanks to a careful selection of all important text passages and the use of clear, easily understandable language. Comments added to the translation will facilitate a deep understanding of this ancient and yet timeless eastern teaching

The author

Until the age of forty, Bernd Helge Fritsch was a successful lawyer in the Austrian city of Graz. Following an inner voice, he gave up his law practice. Since then, he has been active as a writer, spiritual teacher and mentor.

He spent many years travelling, mainly in Asia and southern Europe. He lived in Buddhist and Hindu monasteries, studying and practicing Zen.

In particular his books, "The Jewel of Shankara", "Der große Prinz und das Glück", and "Wu Wei" have made Bernd H. Fritsch well-known among a large circle of readers and as an inspiring author.

Further information about his books, lectures and seminars is available under *www.berndhelgefritsch.com*.

Contents

I. Foreword 10
The uniqueness of the Bhagavad Gita•10; The "essence" of the Gita•11; Access to the Gita•11; Describing the indescribable•12; Western and Eastern way of thinking•13; The practical use•14; True religion has no label•15; Parallels to Christianity•15

II. The symbolism of the Gita 16
Krishna and Arjuna•16; Krishna and Jesus•17; The great epic of Mahabharata •19; The composition of the Gita•19

Chapter 1 – The frame story 21
The Battle of Kurukshetra•21; The events just prior to the battle•21; Arjuna is overcome by compassion•22

Chapter 2 – The everlasting core of Being 24
The difference between transience and the everlasting•24; The Self knows neither birth nor death•24; Reincarnation•25; Selfless action, the basis for liberation•26; Mastery of the mind•26; You deplore what is not deplorable•26; Pleasure and pain•27; The real is everlasting•28; The Self is not born and does not die•28; All phenomena come and go•29; No one knows the Self, the Atman•29; No entitlement to the fruits of your labour•30; Deeply rooted in pure consciousness•31; Control your thoughts•32; Attaining inner peace•33

Chapter 3 – Karma yoga: Oneness with God through the right deeds 34
Karma yoga, Bhakti yoga, Jnana yoga, Raja yoga, Hatha yoga•34; Action and avoiding action•34; The Middle Way•35; Man proposes, God disposes•36; Karma•36; The soul's freedom of choice•37; Karma aims neither at rewards nor at punishment•37; You are not your own destiny•38; Dualist thinking is the problem•39; Recognize the "kingdom of heaven" within you!•39; The necessity of acting•40; Selfless acting•41; Follow the voice of your heart!•41; Set an example!•42; You are not the doer•43; Likes and dislikes•43

Chapter 4 – Jnana yoga - the way of recognition 45

There is an "Avatar" hidden within everyone•43; Non-action in action•45; Contentment•46; Liberation from karma•47; The timeless Krishna•47; Recognize the divine Self!•48; Stay independent of your own action!•49; Awareness of God•50; Wisdom is the highest goal•50; Guilt and karma will burn•51; Mastering the senses•51

Chapter 5 – Self-denial and the yoga of action 52

Karma yoga or Sannyasa•52; Non-identification•53; Renouncing the joys of life?•53; Untouched like a lotus leaf•55; Recognition liberates•55; Serenity and contentment•56; Finding your inner light•56

Chapter 6 – Controlling our mind, and meditation (Raja yoga) 58

All happiness comes from the bottom of the soul•58; The creative power of thinking•58; Liberation from the compulsion of thought•59; Achieving oneness through self-awareness•60; The nature of meditation•60; The fate of those who do not achieve fulfillment•60; Selfless service•61; Your mind - your greatest friend and enemy•61; Yoga of meditation•62; Finding the right measure•63; The self in all beings•64; Control of the spirit•64; No one who makes an effort will be lost•64

Chapter 7 – God's lower and higher nature 66

Many are called, but few are chosen•66; The two natures of the deity•66; Non-identification•67; The Gunas and the Maya•68; Focus on God•69; The lower and higher nature of God•69; Krishna the seed of everything•70; Seeing through the Maya•71; The Godseekers•71; Man is governed by what he believes•71; Born in illusion•72

Chapter 8 – Death and rebirth 74

Erasing the ego•74; The cycles of the universe (Yugas)•75; The path of light and the path of darkness•75; Brahman, Atman and karma•76; The state of Being after death•76; The supreme Purusha•77; Non-return•77; The day and the night of the Brahma•78; The goal of all goals•78; Two paths beyond the world•78

Chapter 9 – The Royal Knowledge (Raja Vidya) 80
Eternal life•80; All is Brahman•81; The human ego nature•81; I am the way and the life•82; No one is preferred•82; God is not identical to his creatures•83; Ignorance causes ego thinking•83; Taking part in the nature of the deity•84; The inner observer•85; Worshiping other gods•86; Always be connected with divine oneness•86; Seeking refuge within the inner God•87

Chapter 10 – The power and the glory of God 88
Krishna the creator of all worlds•88; Krishna and his revelations•88; I am the sun among the heavenly bodies•89; The origin of all phenomena•89; Krishna's glory•90; Krishna grants his wish and explains•91

Chapter 11 – Arjuna's vision 93
Arjuna "beholds" the highest deity•93; The Apocalypse•93; All happens according to Gods plan•93; Your decision•94; Krishna's thousand fold forms•94; The supreme truth•95; The fate of the warriors is predetermined•96; Seeing and worshiping the deity in all things•97

Chapter 12 – Bhakti yoga or the connection with the absolute 98
Honour God in the absolute or in his creatures?•98; Serving and enjoying the well-being of all creatures•99; Always keep your mind on me•100; The truly devoted•101

Chapter 13 – The field and the knower of the field 103
Prakriti and Purusha•103; Like two golden birds in a tree•103; The differentiation between the Self and nature•104; The characteristics of the knowers•105; Brahman, goal of all goals•106; Nature and the Self •106; Liberation•107; All that happens is a play of nature•108

Chapter 14 – The three Gunas: Rajas, Tamas, Sattva 109
The Gunas, the "stuff" of life•109; How the three Gunas are shaping the mind•109; Duality and individuality•110; Meaning of the earthly life - the ego phase•111; Longing for oneness•111; Lib-

eration of the soul•111; Brahman and Brahma •112; The three Gunas determine nature•113; Identification with the body and the mind•113; Merger with the Self through non-identification•114; Reposing - in joy and sorrow•115

Chapter 15 – Jiva - the soul of man ... 116
The World Tree•116; Jiva, the soul of man•116; Identification with the manifest person•117; The dualist view of man•118; The sword of non-adherence•118; Overcoming duality•119; Birth of the soul•119; Walk resolutely on the path of yoga•120; I am the light of the sun•120; The highest Self (Purushottama) •121

Chapter 16 – Divine and demonic characteristics ... 122
"Good" and "evil" persons•122; The struggle against evil•123; The characteristics of those connected with God•123; Demonic characteristics•124

Chapter 17 – The Gunas in all spheres of life ... 126
The power of faith•126; The Gunas and man's behaviour•126; Om Tat Sat•126; Man is what his faith is•127; Types of askesis•128

Chapter 18 – Denial and liberation ... 130
Action or non-action•130; The difference between castes•130; Conditions for becoming one with Brahman•131; Recognition, acting, reason and perseverance•131; Sattva joy•132; Perform the tasks that fit your own nature•132; Achieving oneness with Brahman•131; The Lord directs all movements•133; Give up all religions•134

Conclusion – The essence of the Gita ... 135
The deity within you •135; Blasphemy•136; Ego and being God•137; Wise men live beyond dualist evaluation•137; The imperfection of the dualist world•138; Breaking through things•138;

Index ... 140

Recommended books ... 143

I. Foreword

The uniqueness of the Bhagavad Gita

In its philosophical and spiritual clarity and its comprehensive presentation, the *Bhagavad Gita* cannot be compared to any other teachings handed down to us from antiquity. In it, we find all *Hindu* teachings in a nutshell that were meaningful at the time of its origin. All important questions of earthly and divine concern are fully dealt with in this Gita (Song) of Bhagavad (the Sublime).

The probably best known hymn of praise composed for the Gita in western culture comes from the great explorer and statesman Wilhelm von Humboldt (1767-1935):

"I thank God that He let me live long enough to learn of this book, the most beautiful, perhaps the only true philosophical poem existing in any literature known to us."

Dr. Sarvepalli Radhakrishnan, formerly professor of comparative religion and ethics at Oxford University, was perhaps the most influential commentator of the Gita in modern times. He was president of India from 1962 to 1967 (an amazing exception: a spiritual teacher of wisdom at the head of a gigantic state). In his introduction to the Gita he wrote:

"Through centuries, millions of Hindus have found comfort in this book which presents the basic principles of a spiritual religion in clear, penetrating words, without poorly founded facts, unscientific propositions or even arbitrary phantasies. Even today, as in the long history of its spiritual energy, it still serves those as a beacon of light who want to receive enlightenment from the depth of its wisdom..."

The great philosopher Arthur Schopenhauer (1788-1860) wrote enthusiastically about the Gita:

"Those who have become familiar with this book through diligent reading are deeply touched by its spirit. It is the world's

most educational and sublime teaching. It has been the solace of my life and will be the solace of my death."

The "essence" of the Gita

The Gita, consisting of 18 chapters with 700 verses, was written in Sanskrit, the ancient Indian language regarded as "sacred". Numerous translations exist into just about every language in the world. However, it is not easy for anyone in the West to find a good, easily readable edition of the Gita.

The reasons are in the original with its

- disconcerting way of thinking
- innumerable repetitions
- confusing contradictions
- abstruse religious terminology
- many unknown names from Indian mythology

When we realize how some books that were highly current and have fanned people's imagination one or two hundred years ago, are hardly readable today, or how movies from the time before World War II and from the 1950s and 60s seem completely old-fashioned to us, it is no wonder that today's readers cannot easily comprehend the spiritual message of scripture whose origins go back a few thousand years.

Access to the Gita

The author of this book has studied Asian and Western spirituality for decades. He teaches about Ancient Indian doctrines of wisdom in lectures, university courses and public seminars. In the course of this teaching, he has realized that Western students are finding it difficult to connect with the essential thoughts of the Bhagavad Gita based on reading editions available in bookstores.

He met several people who had come across the Gita and tried to find a deeper understanding of this scripture. Encountering the above difficulties, most had soon given up this attempt.

In writing this version of the Gita, the author's object was to present the wonderfully wise teachings of this scripture in a most easily understandable way. He wanted the Gita to be a readable, interesting text as well as a practical guide for those who - like "Arjuna" - want to walk the path leading to the achievement of their own Self.

On the one hand, the author of this version intended to stay as close as possible with the original text, and on the other hand to remove unimportant and repeated verses which make understanding more difficult. Also, he simplified or left out all together some passages that deal specifically with differences between various philosophical and religious movements or traditions in Ancient India, but do not help us to understand "the essence of the Gita". That is why several of the approximately 700 verses of the Gita are not included in this book.

As a comparison of the numerous translations indicates, the specific characteristics of Sanskrit in conjunction with the verse form in which the Gita is written, provides a large spectrum for different interpretations. That is why all translations and commentaries depend to a great deal on the translator's or commentator's way of thinking. Of course, this also applies to the present "Essence of the Bhagavad Gita".

Describing the indescribable

The main difficulty for the author of a book on the transcendental Being is that he tries to find words for the reality that is beyond our dualist world of terminology. He uses traditional words like "God" or "Brahman", "universal consciousness", "Karma" or "Atman" knowing that they can never express what they represent. They can only serve as signposts to give readers the direction in which their mind must move to learn about the "indescribable". For that reason, teachers of wisdom like to use images and parables to explain the inexpressible. It then depends on the reader's readiness to discover what is substantial behind the words.

As we can recognize especially well in the Gita, when spiritual teachers explain something, they like to step down occasionally from their own non-dualist consciousness level to the pupil's mental level and then climb back to their own higher dimension. This reflects their effort to get the pupil away from the consciousness level on which he happens to be. This procedure explains occasional contradictions in the statements of these spiritual masters.

Western and Eastern way of thinking

To accept the Bhagavad Gita not only with the mind, but also as a whole human being - with heart and soul - it is necessary to open our mind to the special way in which Asian "seers" (Rishis) think.

Western thought works primarily on the analytical level of dualist reasoning. According to our logic, something is either true or false, good or evil. As a rule, for us the "evil" cannot be something "good" at the same time. The Western mind thinks that on the one hand opposites exclude each other, and that on the other hand they may exist independently of each other, that the good can destroy the evil, after which there will only be the good. To Asian philosophers (lovers of wisdom!) this way of thinking is absurd. To them, the evil depends on the good and vice versa; the evil ends only beyond good and evil.

Spiritual teachers of Hinduism, Zen Buddhism and other Eastern spiritual currents have another kind of access to truth. Usually Westerners need time to get used to that way of thought and expression, for it includes possibilities beyond dualist reason which seem illogical, paradox and incomprehensible to Western minds.

For the "Rishis" there is - in addition to the opposites of good and evil - a Being that extends beyond those two.
- They recognize a divine completeness that includes and harbours all opposites and inconsistencies.
- In addition to the past, present and future time, they also know a "timeless" time.
- They know of a "life" without birth or death.
- They achieve a "love" that includes all Being.
- For them, an individual "Being God" (Atman) exists which is also identical to the universal deity (Brahman).

What Western man calls the "real world" is a fantastic illusion to the wise men of the East. On the other hand, what the Rhisis call "reality" does not exist at all for the Western intellect. That "reality" can only be comprehended beyond the dualist patterns of thought.

The practical use

What practical use can we expect from studying the Bhagavad Gita which - next to the Bible - is regarded as the most widely distributed book worldwide?

We find answers to mankind's most important questions:
- Is there a God? And if yes, who, how and where is God?
- Who am I? What is the relationship between my soul and God?
- What causes my joys and my sorrows?
- What is the meaning of my life? What is my most important and highest goal?
- How can I overcome worries and suffering, old age, illness and death?
- How can I achieve love while being deeply and lastingly happy?

The Gita provides us with answers to the most important questions about being human. These answers are surprisingly satisfying, full of wisdom and also practically feasible. However, they require that we earnestly and energetically deal with their message. To reach the "goal of goals" requires gradual development as well as mental and spiritual effort.

Every human has all the prerequisites for being successful. However, just as you can only become a good pianist by committing yourself firmly to absorbing the spirit of the music and to practice certain skills, you will also clearly understand the laws of life and become a "master" of joy, love and freedom with the appropriate commitment and a willingness to learn. I hope that my remarks in this book will serve to motivate and support you.

True religion has no label

The spiritual teachings of the Gita are naturally embedded in the religious culture of Ancient India. They were influenced by thoughts from the Vedas and Upanishads, the philosophy of the Samkhya and the instructions of yoga. The Gita not only fully represents the circle of Hinduism's ideas at the time, but also the essence of all religions. This essence is not "Hindu". True religion has no label, no name. It is not Jewish or Christian or Islamic. True religion is what connects people's innermost feelings with the spirit of the visible and invisible universe!

Parallels to Christianity

It is expected that this "Essence of the Gita" will be read mainly by people of Western culture and tradition. Among them will be many who are shaped by the Christian body of thought. For that reason, I have cited some Bible passages and Christian mentors to build a bridge between Ancient Indian wisdom and Christianity. These will clearly show readers how much the great religions coincide in their basic concept. They will also show that those who look for the deepest insight do not need to confess to any particular religion or leave their present religious denomination.

Foreword

II. The symbolism of the Gita

Krishna and Arjuna

It cannot be answered today whether Krishna - who in the Gita acts as the highest God and teacher of wisdom - can be related to any historical person. In any event, he is surrounded by many tales as a sage and Avatar (God who bodily appeared on earth).

The Gita's description of the belligerent conflict and of the two protagonists, Krishna and Arjuna, should be mainly understood as an allegory. This is already clear from the first verse in Chapter 1. There, even the "Kuru battlefield", where according to the epic of Mahabharata the battle took place, is called the "Dharma field" (Sanskrit: dharma kshetra). The term "dharma" is of central importance in Hinduism and Buddhism. In short, dharma can be translated as divine order, justice or meaning of life.

In figurative terms, this war described in the Gita is the conflict between the forces of light and dark within the human soul. Victory of the "good" forces consists of incorporating the divine in the depth of our own soul and thus ending the entanglement with transient manifestations.

The chariot in which Krishna and Arjuna are holding the dialogue symbolizes the body of every human being. It serves as the "vehicle" (tool) during life on earth.

Arjuna can be regarded as representing "normal" man in whom the self-centered interests of the ego are active. His soul is fixed upon the world's phenomena which provide him with temporary joy, but in the long run with much suffering. His soul does not recognize the meaning of its life journey and is without reference to the forces acting beyond the senses.

Initially, Arjuna refuses to "kill" his "friends and relatives", which stands for giving up his ego, his beloved vanities, his passions, anxieties and wishes because he identifies himself with them; they represent "his life".

Krishna "the charioteer" can be regarded as a symbol of the Self (Sanskrit: Atman), man's divine essential core. He handles the horses of the chariot. He symbolizes man's power to direct his mental energies (thinking, feeling and wanting) toward the right goal.

Thus Krishna is the hidden "charioteer and master" of our body and mind. He represents the universal (divine) wisdom and love acting deeply within every person. In other cultures this master is called the Christ or the Buddha "within us". He shows us, if we listen to him, the way to our supreme destiny.

Therefore, the figure of Krishna as we meet him in the Bhagavad Gita, can be understood in two different ways:

First as Avatar, the incarnation of the supreme divinity (Brahman) whose mission is to give man the impulse and support to achieve his own divine core of Being (Atman).

Secondly Krishna symbolizes the divinity which lives as Self (Atman) "in the heart of every human being".

Thus at the bottom of our soul, we are all of one nature with Krishna the charioteer, who speaks to Arjuna in the Gita. We are all by destination a divinity, a centre of conscious Being. We are created in "the image of God" as the Bible calls it *(Genesis 1:26-27)*, but in most people, this divine nature is still waiting to be fulfilled.

Krishna and Jesus

In the Hindu religion, *"Krishna"* plays a similar role as *"Jesus"* in Christianity. He is regarded as the incarnation of *Vishnu*, the highest deity. According to legend, Krishna is born by a virgin *(Devaki)*, just as Jesus. Like Jesus, he is persecuted shortly after his birth by enemies who fear to lose their power and have the intention to kill him.

Foreword

As the Bhagavad Gita tells us, Krishna revealed his divinity to man, explaining what has to be done to be without earthly sadness, to achieve eternal life. In the same way, centuries later, the gospels described the deeds of Jesus.

Even today, both are regarded as the epitome of love, compassion and peace. Both have performed various miracles, have healed illnesses and were able to awaken in others much devotion and readiness of succession.

In the end, both Krishna and Jesus died a violent death: Christ on the cross and Krishna by the arrow of a hunter. Both became the starting point for religious movements.

Both Christ and Krishna had the same message:

> *Love your neighbour and recognize your true divine Being in which all creatures together are the "one".*

Both teachers of wisdom had essentially the same revelation: "God, the kingdom of heaven, is within you!"

> *Luke 17: 20-21 Being asked by the Pharisees when the kingdom of God would come, he answered them, "The kingdom of God is not coming in ways that can be observed;*
>
> *Nor will they say, 'Look, here it is!' or, 'There it is!' For behold, the kingdom of God is within you!"*
>
> *Gita 10:20 Krishna: I am the Self which dwells in the heart of all creatures. I am the beginning, the middle and the end of all beings.*

The parallels between the Ancient Indian stories about Krishna and the story of Jesus Christ as told in the gospels are undeniable. It is very likely that substantial parts of the Jesus story and philosophy were taken from stories about Krishna, which are older by more than a thousand years, and adapted to the religious culture of the Jews and the historical situation in Judea, then part of the Roman Empire.

This is also expressed in the legend of the Magi who came to the birth place of Jesus "from the east" to bring gifts of gold, frankincense and myrrh *(Luke 2:1-11)*. Gold symbolized wisdom, frankincense (which was used as a medicinal herb) symbolized healing, and myrrh (which was used for embalming) symbolized "eternal life"

Of course, this circumstance does not diminish the value of the pearls of wisdom we find in the gospels.

The great epic of Mahabharata

It is astonishing that the story of an imminent bloody belligerent conflict served as the framework for a most spiritual topic of instruction. Apparently the author of the Gita was concerned to make his philosophical work accessible to the broadest possible public. As some scholars believe, he made the setting coincide with the time immediately prior to the battle of the Kurukshetra to insert the teachings of the Gita into the folk epic of Mahabharata, which was very popular in Ancient India. So successful was this chess move that the Gita is still venerated in India today as the most important holy scripture and is regarded - apart from the Bible - as the most widely distributed spiritual book worldwide.

The imminent battle, with the expected death of thousands of warriors, was also a suitable subject for introducing the philosophy of the Gita, which deals with birth and death, the meaning of life, with God and all major issues of life.

The composition of the Gita

The Gita was probably written between the fifth and second centuries B.C. As mentioned, the considerably older philosophical teachings of the Vedas - believed to have originated about a thousand years earlier - were absorbed in the Gita.

The author of the Bhagavad Gita is unknown. According to legend, it was "Vyasa", a sage of Ancient India, also venerated as the incarnation of the God Vishnu. He is also said to be the author of the great Indian heroic epic, the Mahabharata. As mentioned above, the Bhagavad Gita was merged into that epic.

Chapter 1 – The frame story

The Battle of Kurukshetra

The first chapter of the Gita does not have much to do with the content of the spiritual teaching in the following chapters. It serves as an introduction which tells how it happened that Krishna revealed all his wisdom and glory to his pupil Arjuna.

We hear about an event which according to legend took place a long time ago in Ancient India in a field called Kurukshetra. The story refers directly to the feud between two royal families as described in detail in the epic Mahabharata.

In the beginning of the Gita's first chapter, the armies of the "Pandavas" on the one side and the "Kauravas" on the other side are facing each other as enemies, just before a great battle begins. The issue is: Who will rule over the kingdom of "Bharata"?

The Pandavas are led by Prince Arjuna and his four brothers. They are considered kind, serene and righteous. According to the law, Arjuna's oldest brother should be rightful successor to the kingdom's throne. But he and his brothers are persecuted by their relatives, the princes of the Kurus led by Duryodhana. They want to hold on to their illegally assumed power and destroy the Pandavas. Duryodhana and his brothers are described as greedy and evil.

Krishna is the driver of the chariot with which Arjuna will go into the imminent battle. But it is soon discovered that Krishna, a good friend of Arjuna before, is no ordinary charioteer. He reveals himself as the supreme deity who has appeared on earth in human form.

The events just prior to the battle

To understand the essence of the Gita, it is not necessary to know the verses of the first chapter, which describe the situ-

Chapter 1 - The frame story

ation at the Kurukshetra. We are therefore satisfied with a greatly abbreviated description of the scene which leads to the actual content of the Gita:

Verses *1:2-11* describe how before the battle, Prince Duryodhana, leader of the Kauravas, inspects the ranks of the enemies and those of his own men. Many names of famous men who play a role in Indian myths and legends are mentioned.

It is also described how - as was apparently customary at the time - sea shells and cow horns are sounded and drums are beaten to encourage the own men and to intimidate the enemy. This causes a great noise to echo on the battlefield.

Then the scene changes to Arjuna who stands upright in his chariot, speaking to his charioteer Krishna:

> *1:21-23 O Krishna, drive my chariot between the two armies so that I can see who will take part in the battle. I want to see who is lending support to the bad Duryodhana.*
>
> *1:25 So Krishna drove the magnificent chariot between the two armies where he stopped and said: Arjuna, look at all the Kurus assembled here.*
>
> *1:26-27 Here between the two armies, standing in the chariot, Arjuna saw among the enemies fathers and grandfathers, teachers, uncles and brothers, sons, grandsons, other relatives and friends.*

Arjuna is overcome by compassion

At that moment, Arjuna despairs about his mission. He is overtaken by great compassion and begins to lament:

Chapter 1 - The frame story

> *1:28-30 As I see my own relatives here, ready for battle, my limbs grow weak; my mouth runs dry, my body is shaking and my hair stands on end, my skin burns, I lose control of my bow. I cannot stand upright, and all is turning in my head.*
>
> *1:31 I see no sense in killing my relatives in battle, O Krishna. I desire neither victory nor dominion nor other joys.*
>
> *1:32-35 What use to us is kingship, enjoyment and life when all the teachers, fathers, sons and relatives opposing each other here must lose their lives? Even though they may kill me, I am not prepared to kill, not even for all the riches of heaven and earth.*

Chapter 1 ends with those words:

> *1:47 After Arjuna had spoken thus, he threw away bow and arrows and sat down in the chariot, overcome by pain.*

Chapter 2 – The everlasting core of Being

We could say that the verses of this chapter already anticipate the entire philosophy of the Gita in concise form.

The difference between transience and the everlasting

Krishna responds to Arjuna's anxieties and worries and begins his lecture by saying: *"You deplore those who are not deplorable and you believe to speak wise words..."* (2:11). He means that there is no duality of coming and going beyond the dimension of sensory perception. Yet men who trust only their senses do not recognize the reality behind things. They know only the world of transient manifestations. They adhere to it and worry whether they can acquire and keep what they want and love. Those who perceive only the transient will necessarily be plagued by anxiety and worries - consciously or subconsciously.

People's problems result from ignorance. They do not know that their soul is indestructible. They do not know the meaning of their earthly journey. They do not know that their soul wanders from incarnation to incarnation until it has reached the goal of all those embodiments.

The Self knows neither birth nor death

In Verses *2:19-24*, Krishna tries to show that man is not identical to his body and his actions. The depth of man's soul, his Self, his true essence, is never born or destroyed.

As explained in Verse *2:19*, there is no man who can be killed, and no one should believe that he could kill someone. These words only make sense if we distinguish between the mortal body and the immortal soul.

Chapter 2 - The everlasting core of Being

Reincarnation

Every soul dwells in a body during its presence on earth. As Verse *2:22* relates, it discards this body like old clothes as soon as it can no longer perform its task as a "tool", and acquires a new body. As Verse *15:8* also describes wonderfully: *"...the soul, as it leaves the body, takes along the strength of the senses and of the organ of thought, bringing it along when it merges with another body again."*

In Hinduism and Buddhism it is self-evident that every soul passes through innumerable embodiments. This gives it the opportunity to achieve higher and higher levels of consciousness.

The Ancient Greek philosophers such as Socrates and Plato were also convinced of that. In early Christendom, the reincarnation doctrine was widespread, especially thanks to the influence of the Greek philosophers. Later, the majority of Christian church fathers opposed it because they regarded it as incompatible with the idea that all the dead will be resurrected on Judgement Day.

According to Hindu and Buddhist teachings, the ego's unfulfilled wishes and desires cause the soul to find a new body after death, to satisfy its needs.

The conditions under which man is reborn depend on the karma he has caused in his previous life. His thinking and acting in the old life determine in what body, with what mental and spiritual assets, with what parents and in what environment he will appear on earth again to continue developing his soul.

Yet those who at the time of death are connected with the bliss of Brahman will be liberated from Samsara, the wheel of constant rebirths. His ego and his adherence to the joys of the world have expired even before he died. That is why after leaving his body he is not interested in going through the joys and sorrows again which the world offers.

Chapter 2 - The everlasting core of Being

Selfless action, the basis for liberation

Beginning with Verse *2:39*, the kind and meaning of selfless action are described. The Gita has also been called the "Canticle of action" (K.O. Schmidt) because it emphasizes the necessity of selfless action (Karma yoga).

Those who act unaffected by egotistical desires are on the best way to liberation. He meets his obligations and keeps his composure whether his actions succeed or fail. He does his best, leaving the decision about the fruit of his labour to all-encompassing wisdom. His happiness and peace of mind are unaffected by the way of the world.

Mastery of the mind

Verses *2:58 ff.* describe the conditions under which we can be without problems and worries. One basic requirement is to always carefully observe events in one's own mind. That makes it possible to control these events better and better.

Otherwise the ego will spread out with its likes and dislikes. This will lead to trouble, dependencies, passion, anxiety and confusion *(see Chapter 6)*. On the other hand, those who remain untouched by wishes and expectations will enjoy the love, wisdom and completeness at the bottom of his soul.

The term "mind" is usually defined as a bundle of mental abilities allowing perception, thinking, judging and memory as well as feelings and impulses of will.

You deplore what is not deplorable

> *2:2 Krishna: Where does your weakness come from, Arjuna, in this difficult hour of decision? It is unworthy of you. This is not how you attain higher worlds but you will only earn disgrace.*

> *2:6 Arjuna: I do not know what is better, that we defeat the enemy or that they defeat us.*
>
> *2:7 I am confused, and my strength fails me. Tell me what is the better way! Let me be your pupil!*
>
> *2:8 My sorrow will not end, even if I should win power over all men and gods.*

Arjuna repeats his worries and doubts whether he should take part in this battle.

> *2:10 In the middle between the two armies, Krishna, with a smile on his face, spoke to Arjuna, who had lost himself in his pain.*
>
> *2:11 You deplore those who are not deplorable and believe to speak clever words. But wise men do not complain about the living or the dead.*
>
> *2:12 There never was a time when you and I and the kings and princes assembled here did not exist, nor will there be a time when we cease to exist.*
>
> *2:13 As the soul dwells in the body through childhood, youth and old age, it will find another body after death. Wise men will not be disturbed by such changes.*

Krishna points out that man's body only serves as his temporary residence while he dwells on earth. Man is not identical to his body. The soul is not "born" when it is incarnated and it does not cease to exist when the body dies.

Pleasure and pain

> *2:14 Sensory perception leads to pleasure or pain. These experiences come and go like summer and winter. Learn to endure them patiently, Arjuna!*
>
> *2:15 Those who remain serene in the face of pleasure and pain are truly wise and will achieve liberation.*

Chapter 2 - The everlasting core of Being

Life in a body is unavoidably connected with pleasant and unpleasant experiences. The wise man meets these experiences with serenity and always remains in touch with his higher Self.

The real is everlasting

> *2:16 What is transient has no reality. The real never stops to be. Those who learn to differentiate between these two and realize their meaning have attained wisdom.*
>
> *2:17 Recognize the indestructible nature of what causes and permeates the phenomena! Who is to destroy this unchangeable and everlasting spirit?*
>
> *2:18 The body is mortal. But incomprehensible and everlasting is the Self that dwells in the body. Therefore, go and fight in this battle, Arjuna!*

Those who have recognized the everlasting self no longer mourn the loss of the transient. They recognize the coming and going of bodies as a play that is directed by a wise divine hand to lead man to a higher consciousness.

The Self is not born and does not die

> *2:19 He is ignorant who looks upon himself as the killer and the other as the killed. What you really are does not kill nor can it be killed.*
>
> *2:20 The Self was never born and will never die. What you really are will never cease to exist. Unborn, eternal, unchangeable, you will not die although your body perishes.*
>
> *2:21 How can the Self, which is recognized as an indestructible, unborn and everlasting Being, be killed by anyone?*

> *2:22 Just as a man discards clothes that have become unusable and acquires new ones, the Self will acquire a new body once the old body no longer suits.*
>
> *2:24 The Self is everlasting and all-permeating. It can never be destroyed. It is described as invisible, inconceivable and unchangeable.*

In almost all chapters, the Gita continuously deals with the Self, man's immortal core of Being that cannot be perceived with the senses. This Self, usually called "Atman" in Sanskrit, must be recognized and fulfilled to liberate itself from the cycle of rebirths and to acquire eternal life.

All phenomena come and go

> *2:26 Even though you assume that the soul is subject to birth and death again and again, you should not complain.*
>
> *2:27 Death is inevitable for those who were born; birth is inevitable for the dead. What is there to mourn?*
>
> *2:28 All creatures are concealed in the beginning, then they become apparent, and in the end they are concealed again. So why should you be sorry?*

We recognize the eternal cycle of coming and going in nature. All things and creatures we can see are subject to that. Those who have recognized the eternal self are untouched by this.

No one knows the Self, the Atman

> *2:29 Some regard the Self as a mystery. Others hear or speak of it as a miracle. Yet no one who merely heard of it can recognize it.*
>
> *2:30 The Self dwells in every body. It is eternal and indestructible. Therefore you should not worry.*

Chapter 2 - The everlasting core of Being

There are no words to describe the Self, and the mind alone cannot understand it. Consciously realizing the Self, we can "behold" it or - even better - "live" it. The Gita explains the conditions in detail.

> *2:31 You should not waver in your duty as a warrior (Kshatriya). It is necessary for a warrior to engage in the fight against evil.*
>
> *2:33 If you do not take up this fight for justice, you neglect your duty. You will become guilty, and you will lose your reputation as a warrior.*
>
> *2:38 Happiness and sorrow, loss and gain, victory and defeat should not touch your soul. If you act with that attitude, you will not bear the burden of guilt.*

Krishna reminds Arjuna to do his duty as a member of the warrior caste. To add weight to his meaning, he steps down to Arjuna's level of dualist consciousness and refers to guilt and disgrace, should he fail to do his duty. In later verses, he explains that a wise man whose level of consciousness is higher will remain unaffected by praise and reproach *(see 12:18)*.

No entitlement to the fruits of your labour

> *2:47 Take care that you do your duty. Yet the fruits of your labour should not be your motivation.*
>
> *2:48 Do your duty without demands and rejection. Remain unaffected by success and failure. Such composure is called yoga.*
>
> *2:49 Deeds are worth less than the curbing of reason. Therefore find refuge in reason. Poor are those who strive for the fruits of their labour.*

We repeatedly read in the Gita that spiritual progress is possible only if we perform our tasks selflessly without greedily looking for the fruits of our labour. Such action prevents karmic entanglements. We should do our best to perform our duties and then leave it up to the universal spirit whether success will follow.

In this respect, Mahatma Gandhi recommended an *"absolutely detached and yet absolutely committed"* inner attitude.

Deeply rooted in pure consciousness

> *2:50 Those whose mind rests in oneness will go beyond the dualist judgement of "good" and "bad". They will do neither good nor evil deeds. Therefore strive for this clarity of yoga.*

By nature, man is endowed with a dualist consciousness. It means we necessarily think in contrasts of "good" and "bad", "pleasant" and "unpleasant", "I want - I don't want". We live in duality, separated from the divine, all-encompassing "oneness". To become one with the Self and with all Being, we must advance into the consciousness dimension beyond dualist thinking and judging. According to the Gita, this becomes possible through the yoga paths. They will be described in detail in the later verses.

> *2:51 The wise men, who have become one with the Self, forego the fruits of their labour. Thus they are liberated from the shackles of rebirth and reach the place beyond all misery.*
>
> *2:52 When your spirit has gone beyond the illusion of duality, you will remain in a state of composure to all that happens.*

Chapter 2 - The everlasting core of Being

> 2:55 One who has given up all selfish desires, who finds fulfillment in the Self, is rooted in pure consciousness.
>
> 2:56 He will be called firmly rooted in his spirit who is neither shaken by suffering nor carried away by joy and who is without adherence, fear and rage.

The dualist perspective produces a greatly distorted view of reality. To overcome this illusion of duality, man has to go beyond his ego. This ego is characterized by obsessive thoughts, greed, selfishness, anger, anxiety and worries *(see Chapter 14 for details)*.

> 2:57 Those who are without desire, who neither rejoice when met by pleasure nor complain when met by displeasure, are firmly rooted in knowledge.

The wise see through the relative value and the perishability of all things and events. That is why their peace of mind is not disturbed.

Control your thoughts

> 2:58 Those who like a tortoise retract their limbs in a shell and keep their mind off external objects, are regarded as firmly rooted in true knowledge.
>
> 2:61 Those who control their senses, thoughts and feelings and always keep their mind on the Self are regarded as deeply rooted in consciousness.
>
> 2:62 Thinking of sensual objects commits us to them. This restraint leads to desires, and desire leads to passion.
>
> 2:63 Passion leads to confusion. Confusion is followed by loss of memory (of the Self). This destroys our reason and ruins us.
>
> 2:64 When you are without adherence and aversion, all worries will end, and deep inner peace will follow.

> 2:66 Those who do not control their thought will find no peace. They cannot remain in concentration. Yet how can there be happiness without inner peace?

Attaining inner peace

> 2:69 What is night to all creatures is the light of day for the wise, and what all creatures regard as being awake is dark night to those who are enlightened.

The ignorant do not know the bliss of the Self. To them, the transcendent is like the darkness of night. For the wise, the connection with the Self is supreme bliss.

To the ignorant, the illusions of dualist thinking are the only reality. The wise on the other hand consider them "dark night".

> 2:70 Just as the great ocean is not moved by the waters that constantly enter it, those will remain calm who observe the flood of desires and rejection with composure and without being touched.
>
> 2:71 Those who are without selfishness, who desire nothing and act freely will attain deep peace.
>
> 2:72 This, Arjuna, is divine and eternal life. Those who attain it will no longer be confused. Those who in their hour of death are deeply rooted in that state will enter the kingdom of God (brahma nirvana).

Chapter 3 – Karma yoga: Oneness with God through the right deeds

Karma yoga, Bhakti yoga, Jnana yoga, Raja yoga, Hatha yoga

In the third chapter of the Gita, the path to liberation and oneness with the deity through selfless action (Karma yoga) is described. Literally, the Sanskrit term "karman" means action or deed. It was envisioned in Ancient India that every deed is closely connected with its consequences. Therefore, karma also means the fate resulting from the deeds.

The term "yoga" comes from the Sanskrit word "yuga", the yoke. The word has innumerable meanings. In Hinduism, it is also used as the connection with the highest deity. According to Ancient Indian wisdom, there are many paths to reach this oneness. The most important are Karma yoga (yoga of action), Bhakti yoga (yoga of devotion), Jnana yoga (yoga of recognition) and Raja yoga (King's yoga, yoga through mastering the mind). In the western world, yoga became known mainly in the form of Hatha yoga. That path concentrates on physical exercises (asanas), breathing exercises (pranayamas) and meditation.

Action and avoiding action

Arjuna, who is not willing to take part in the imminent belligerent conflict, asks Krishna why he is urging him to participate in the battle when mastering the mind is more important than acting. He refers to Krishna's remark according to which deeds are worth considerably less than controlling the mind *(2:49)*.

He thus gives Krishna reason to deal more closely with the subject of "selfless action" and "avoiding action".

Krishna explains that action is inevitable for the incarnate soul. It is only the requirements of the body that force it to act.

Completeness is not reached by denying action and practicing strict asceticism. In this, Krishna is referring to the Ancient Indian tradition by which the Self can be achieved through extreme abstinence and abandoning all worldly life.

The Middle Way

It was said that the Gautama Buddha left the splendour of his father's royal palace after he recognized the suffering of mankind. For six years he practiced harsh asceticism in solitude to achieve inner liberation. He ended this after he realized the uselessness of this self-denial and announced the "Middle Way" between the two extremes of asceticism and dependence on sensual indulgence.

Thus spoke Buddha in the Sermon of Benares:

> *"Two extremes, bhikkhus (monks), should not be practiced by the homeless. What are these two? In material matters, to adhere to the material well-being - to the lower, common, ordinary, ignoble and hopeless; and devotion to self-torture, to the painful, the ignoble and the hopeless. Avoiding these two extremes, the completed one has been awakened to the Middle Way which leads to serenity, to an overview, an awakening - to Nirvana."*

In the Gita, the term "not adhering to passions" is emphasized again and again as an important prerequisite for all yoga ways. This does not mean we must turn our back on external life. The Gita does not say we must go into homelessness or live as a begging monk to be a Sannyasa (in self-denial). The deciding factor is our inner attitude while acting. If we act selflessly in close connection with our Self, we will remain untouched by our deeds emotionally and also karmically.

Chapter 3 - Karma yoga: Oneness with God through the right deeds

Man proposes, God disposes

In Verses *3:27-30*, Krishna explains that all events on earth are guided by God's forces of nature (Prakriti). But *"...man, confused by his ego feeling, thinks he makes the decisions."*

Man, identifying with his body and his mind (thinking, feeling, wanting), thinks that his "I" makes decisions freely and acts freely. The Gita contradicts him and explains that man's thinking and wanting is governed largely by the Gunas *(see Chapter 14)*.

Those who carefully observe themselves and other people will soon discover that the kind of decisions we make depends on our predisposition (genes), our upbringing, habits and the culture in which we live. This leaves little room for "free will".

However: The less we adhere to our ego wishes and the more open we are for our divine core of Being, the more wisdom and freedom we achieve. We then live our individual deity (Atman) which is one with the universal consciousness (Brahman). Thus we will ourselves become a creative force incorporated in the actions of the highest deity. Like a musician in a great orchestra we will play our very own instrument while acting as part of the whole.

Karma

Verse *3:31* addresses the subject of fate (karma). This is how the law of karma can be described briefly:

> *"Good deeds have good consequences, evil deeds have evil consequences - deeds just for the sake of doing will have no consequences at all!"*

As long as a soul has not awakened, it will be governed by the constraints of dualist thinking (ego) and perform "good" as well as "bad" deeds.

Such a soul will act the way it has been shaped by its genes, its upbringing and the culture in which it is developing. Without understanding those connections, we can hardly make people responsible for their way of thinking and acting.

This is also what Jesus meant when he said:

> *"Father, forgive them, for they do not know what they are doing."* *(Luke 23:34)*

The soul's freedom of choice

In spite of all ignorance, the universe continually gives the soul an opportunity to decide either on the "ego way" or to connect with its "divine inside". Typical for the ego way is the search for external happiness, for love we expect from others, for money and power. This leads to anger, anxieties, doubts and worries. The other way, the way to the Self, leads to inner peace, to love that gives and wants to receive nothing, to complete happiness.

Several times a day we are called upon to choose whether we want to worry and let external circumstances oppress us, or whether we want to stop identifying ourselves with our body, our mind and the circumstances of our life.

Every day, the soul is given several chances to take at least a small step in one or another direction. According to the law of karma, these decisions determine our future well-being, our health and out future destiny.

Thus, our soul does have room for deciding freely in addition to being coordinated by karma, by our disposition and our upbringing. It is responsible for the karmic consequences resulting from our decisions and actions.

Karma aims neither at rewards nor at punishment

Karma, with its pleasant and unpleasant consequences, should not be regarded as award or punishment. In the "reality" of the universe, there is no punishing God, only wisdom and love. Karma belongs to the divine play of Maya (the great illusion). Fate only serves to shake us awake from the dream of "good" and "evil". If the proper insight is achieved at the end of an often very long way, the soul goes beyond the bond with its destiny. It "crosses the sea of guilt" and reaches the shore of its Self *(see 4:36-37)*.

You are not your own destiny

Fate determines people's lives as long as they do not recognize the real nature of life. Karma exists only on man's dualist level of consciousness. The law of karma is part of the dream, the great illusion (Maya) in which man usually exists. Karma ends for those who

- don't identify with their body, their thinking and feeling,
- live in the "here and now" without having unnecessary thoughts about the past and the future,
- wake up from the dualist thoughts of "good" and "evil" and recognize the completeness of Being.

Karma always just affects our body and our mind (thinking, feeling, wanting). The Self (Atman) is touched neither by good nor by bad karma. There are no dualist distinctions for the Self. The Self lives in complete harmony with what is. And what is, is God. There is no "good" and "bad" on that level of consciousness *(see 5:15-17)*.

Those who recognize their Self are liberated from the endless chain of cause and effect that has determined all their previous incarnations.

All people have a Self and are the Self, and that Self has nothing to do with the problems of ego. The Self is pure consciousness. It contains everything. It is everything, the earth and the sky, plants and animals, and all people. If we recognize this, our personal worries and problems begin to fade like soft mist in the morning sun. It is only a question of recognition and consciousness whether we are beings restrained by karma or liberated and happy.

Dualist thinking is the problem

Man's problem is only his thinking which is concentrating on the world's transient manifestations. We ponder too much whether we are well or not and what will await us in the future. That is the soil on which karma grows.

You think about your problems. That is why you feel badly, stressed, angry, worried, etc. You feel badly when you think about what is bad and that you feel badly. The worries cause the problems, not the other way round! That is how the illusion of karma originates.

The Self, the "pure consciousness" calmly observes what happens. It is like watching a film on a movie screen. Our pure consciousness does not identify with the film that is shown. We look through the illusion of the film and don't worry whether it turns out "well" or "badly". Pure consciousness is connected with the bliss of Being. It lives in the here and now and does what it has to do - period.

Tell yourself again and again, especially when you wake up in the morning: "I am not the transient manifestation of life, I am not my body, my thinking, my feeling. I am pure, everlasting, unlimited, happy and completely aware. All else is a transient play that is being performed on the movie screen of my conscience."

Recognize the "kingdom of heaven" within you!

As told in Verses *3:34* and *3:37-38*, passion, anger and rage result from the misinterpretation of sensory perception. The ignorant do not recognize divine guidance behind all phenomena. Blinded by the wishes of their ego, they assume that creation is not complete. They therefore want to change the world to their own advantage. Often, this results in restless action to achieve external success, power, wealth, recognition and affection.

Others believe they must improve the world "unselfishly". That also results from the confusion of our ego. God does not need helpless helpers. The only thing that makes sense and is generally useful is to find the "kingdom of heaven" (God) within ourselves *(Luke 17:20-21)*. We can best help the world by waking up from ignorance. This will quite naturally lead to loving, harmonious actions in oneness with all beings, without any "must" or "want".

The necessity of acting

> *3:1 Arjuna: If you find the way toward insight more important than acting, why are you urging me to take part in this terrible battle?*
>
> *3:3 Krishna: There are two ways leading to liberation: Jnana yoga - the way of recognition, and Karma yoga - the way of selfless action.*

We all have our own access to higher truth, depending on our individuality. The Gita distinguishes primarily two ways, that of recognition and that of selfless action. These two supplement each other *(see introductions to Chapters 5 and 12)*.

Doing your duty selflessly is the basis for the purity of spirit and for true recognition. Highest recognition leads to the eternal, non-manifested and indescribable Being.

> *3:4 You do not reach completeness by refraining from action in the external world and by living ascetically.*
>
> *3:5 No being can be without action for even a moment. We are forced to act by our own nature.*

Chapter 3 - Karma yoga: Oneness with God through the right deeds

> *3:8 Perform all your duties! Acting is better than not acting. You must act even to maintain the body.*

Selfless acting

> *3:9 In the world, we are forced to perform actions. But act selflessly! Selfish action ties you to the world.*
>
> *3:10 The Lord created man to act selflessly. That was to make him fruitful. That way, he will find that all his wishes will come true.*
>
> *3:12 You will receive all things you need from the gods. But he who enjoys their gifts without giving himself is a thief.*
>
> *3:14 To feed the body, we need rain. It is a gift of nature. It comes to us under the principle of selfless service which works in the universe.*
>
> *3:15-16 Selfless action, Arjuna, has its origin in Brahman, the universal God.*
>
> *Those who do not work in that spirit waste their lives.*

All that man needs in his life he received from the forces that manifest themselves in nature. Through selfless service we show our gratitude and liberate ourselves from the ego's selfishness.

Follow the voice of your heart!

> *3:17 Those who have found their own self are always content. They enjoy their own self. They do not meet any outside obligations but follow the voice of their heart.*
>
> *3:18 They do not desire profit from the outside world. They also have nothing to gain from deeds they may have performed or not.*

> *3:19 Therefore do your duty without paying attention to the results; that is how you will reach fulfillment.*

Contentment leads to inner harmony which creates room for developing completeness, love and bliss for the Self.

Set an example!

> *3:20 Janaka and others achieved the highest levels of consciousness by doing their duty selflessly. That is how you should meet your obligations.*

Janaka was the legendary king of Mithila, a kingdom in the north of India. He is regarded as a great example because he is said to have given up his ego, working for mankind unselfishly.

> *3:21 People rooted within their own self act as examples for others. Ordinary people like to follow in their footsteps.*
>
> *3:22 For me (Krishna) there is nothing to gain in the entire universe, yet I am constantly active.*
>
> *3:23 Even if I were inactive, many people would follow my example.*
>
> *3:24 If I were to stop acting, this world would plunge into chaos. As a result, all people would be doomed to destruction.*
>
> *3:25 The ignorant do their duty because they are driven by desire. The cognizant do their duty with the intention of serving for the good of all.*
>
> *3:26 Those who have achieved enlightenment and who act in the spirit of yoga should motivate others to do the same.*

Chapter 3 - Karma yoga: Oneness with God through the right deeds

Love and selfless action are the foundation of this ephemeral and transcendent world. Those who exclude themselves abandon the fullness and beauty of Being.

You are not the doer

> 3:27 All that happens in the apparent world is performed by the forces of my nature (Prakriti). Yet man, confused by his ego, believes he is the doer.
>
> 3:28 Those who achieve the power to distinguish do not adhere to the phenomena and do not believe they affect anything themselves.
>
> 3:30 Be always aware that all actions are my doing (Krishna). Therefore refrain from personal expectations and act only in conjunction with me.

Those seeking liberation become used to always observe the functions of their own mind. That is how they gain distance from what their mind and their body does and identify less with those processes.

Likes and dislikes

> 3:31 Those who follow my teaching and do not complain will be delivered from their karma (fate). But those who are blind to all wisdom create their own sorrow.

"Normal" people react to things and external events with likes and dislikes. That is how they develop an ego that is marked by wishes, worries and anxieties.

> 3:34 Likes and dislikes lurk behind all sensory perception. Beware of these enemies on your way.

Chapter 3 - Karma yoga: Oneness with God through the right deeds

> *3:37 Passion is caused by selfish desire. It is connected with anger and other evils threatening mankind.*
>
> *3:38 As smoke surrounds the fire, recognition is clouded by passion.*

Selfish desire and action leads us to aberration and makes us slaves. Passion, anger and rage as well as anxiety leads us into great unawareness. This exposes us to the lower forces of nature.

> *3:42 The capacity of sensory perception is powerful, but our organ of thought (Manas) is even mightier. Reason (Buddhi) rules from one step above the organ of thought. Yet the Self (Atman) is superior to all.*
>
> *3:43 Therefore use your Self to rule over your lowly ego and its desires.*

Ancient Indian philosophy distinguishes between the general ability to think (Manas) and the intuitive ability to recognize truth (Buddhi). The word Buddhi comes from budh (awaking). That is why someone "awakened" is called a Buddha.

Chapter 4 – Jnana yoga - the way of recognition

There is an "Avatar" hidden within everyone

In the first verses of this Chapter *(4:1-3)*, Krishna describes how a very long time ago he revealed the "everlasting yoga" (the wisdom he now teaches Arjuna in the Gita) to the Vedic god Vivasvat, who passed it on to Manu, the progenitor of humanity, who in turn instructed Ikshvaku (a monarch in Indian mythology). From there, the teaching was passed on by a long chain of wise masters.

Arjuna wonders how Krishna, who cannot have been born too long ago, could have revealed this teaching in the distant past. Krishna explains to him that not only he himself, but also Arjuna has already gone through innumerable incarnations.

Krishna explains further that he - as an Avatar ("one who descended") - always appears on earth in the form of a special personality when the eternal teaching is in danger of being forgotten.

Strictly speaking, in the core of our soul, every one of us is an Atavar. This core (Atman) is substantially the same as Brahman, the all-encompassing deity. In Ancient Indian wisdom, there is no difference between the Self and the highest deity. With the achievement of the Self, the soul is one with Brahman, and the other way round: by uniting with Brahman, the soul becomes Atman.

Non-action in action

In Verses *4:14-24*, Krishna describes action which has no karmic consequences. Those "do not act by acting" - who free from personal desires and expectations - perform the duties life requires of them.

Chapter 4 - Jnana yoga - the way of recognition

"Non-action" in the sense of the Gita corresponds to a mental attitude. The "abstainer" (Sannyasa) does not remain in inactivity but does his duty cheerfully and selflessly. Without desire or inner defensiveness he feels what action corresponds to the universal will with which he is in harmony.

Because he acts without being attached to the results of his actions, he feels free and independent. He rests happily and contentedly within himself, no matter what results his actions will have.

"Non-acting" people have reached a higher level of consciousness. They know they are one with the origin of all Being. They have found the bliss of being completely contented.

Contentment

When Ramana Maharshi (20th century Indian teacher of wisdom) was asked who God is, he answered after a long silence:

"God is what is."

God cannot be analysed and defined. All attempts in that direction must fail. No religion can claim that the "true God" belongs to it. The fact that there is a God and what He is can be explained this way:

As the world is, the way natural phenomena and humans are, whether "good" or "evil", that is God. There is only God, and we can only experience God if we take and love the world and life the way it is - with all its sunny and shady sides.

If we rebel against what is, we deny the Being. We deny God. It is silly and unreasonable to rebel against and to be angry and worry about "that which is". Doing that, we only harm ourselves, and we change nothing about the Being, the way it is.

Contentment with what is: That is the key to liberation! Contentment means to desire nothing and instead to be grateful for the grand gifts of life.

Those who are content will accept what is and do not harbour any inner resistance against what they do not like. They are free of dualist evaluations in the direction of "good" and "bad". They are without anger, resentment and rage. However, they do not remain passive. When a situation calls for useful action, they act without emotion.

With that attitude their spirit becomes peaceful. Their thoughts stop swirling around in the head, for they have no worries and anxieties about the future. They expect nothing and cannot be disappointed. This peace of mind opens their heart for love, beauty, wisdom, freedom and the completeness of the Self. In that way, they are not restrained by their actions, as Verse *4:22* explains.

Liberation from karma

Verse *4:33* confirms that selfless action, acting from a state of contentment without desire, opens the gate to highest knowledge.

Readers will find two of the most beautiful verses, full of wisdom and comfort, in *4:36-37*. According to those, karma, caused by all our past follies, fades when we cross the sea of past evil aboard the ship of wisdom.

The timeless Krishna

> *4:1-3 Krishna: I revealed the everlasting yoga to Vivasvat. He passed it on to Manu who then taught Ikshvaku. From there, the teaching was passed on and on by great masters until it was lost in time.*
>
> *This age-old yoga I now reveal to you, for you are my devoted pupil and friend.*
>
> *4:4 Arjuna: You were born after Vivasvat's lifetime. How can I understand that you passed this teaching on to him so long ago?*

Chapter 4 - Jnana yoga - the way of recognition

> *4:5 Krishna: You and I have gone through many births, Arjuna. I know them all, but you do not know them.*
>
> *4:6 My true nature is unborn and unchangeable. I am the Lord who lives in all creatures. Through my power I manifest myself in innumerable transient forms.*

Krishna, as the Gita depicts him, has embodied himself of his own free will. Unknowing people, however, as long as they are entangled in the world of phenomena, are born again and again involuntarily, through the power of nature (Sanskrit: Prakriti).

> *4:7 Every time when the Dharma is disintegrating and the purpose of life is forgotten, I manifest myself in special personalities on earth.*
>
> *4:8 I appear on earth to protect the good, to destroy the evil and to re-establish Dharma.*

In this sense, Dharma is to be understood as knowledge of the spiritual laws.

Recognize the divine Self!

> *4:9 Those who recognize my divine nature and my work will not be born again after their physical death.*
>
> *4:10 Saved from selfish adherence, anxiety and anger, filled by me, devoted to me, cleansed by the fire of my nature, many have achieved the state of oneness with me.*
>
> *4:11 I accept them in my love as they come to me. All ways lead to me.*

By abandoning all peculiarities of the ego, man attains oneness with the deity. At the same time, he achieves his Self (his own divine nature).

Chapter 4 - Jnana yoga - the way of recognition

Stay independent of your own action!

> 4:14 I do not lose myself in my labour and I do not adhere to its fruits. Those who understand this and act likewise will remain independent.

The wise man knows what to do. He works neither too much nor too little. He always remains the composed spectator and does not identify himself with the activities of his body and his mind.

> 4:16 What is acting and what is not acting? Even those far advanced are confused by this question.
>
> 4:17 We should understand what is acting, what is not acting and what is wrong acting.
>
> 4:18 Those who achieve acting in non-acting and non-acting in acting will be without burden and stay within the Self.

"Acting in non-acting and non-acting in acting" is a clever game of words. It means that those who do their duty selflessly do not cause karma by their action. By not selfishly worrying about the success of actions, but leaving the results of labour to the will of the deity, they will not be affected by their activities. They will always do their duty cheerfully and in composure.

> 4:19 Wise are those who act without selfish motives. All their desires and thus also their karma will be burned in the fire of knowledge.
>
> 4:20 In their well-being, they are always contented, without expectations, not dependent on the fruits of their labour. They don't act although they are occupied.
>
> 4:21 Since they are not driven by desires, they master their thinking, their feeling and their wanting. They do not strive for possessions. Thy do not burden themselves with karma.

Chapter 4 - Jnana yoga - the way of recognition

Awareness of God

> 4:22 Those live in freedom who are content with what fate has in store for them. Those who are not concerned about dualist opposites (joy and suffering), who desire nothing and remain the same whether successful or not, will not be restrained by their actions.
>
> 4:23 Those who do not adhere to phenomena, who are self-confident and dedicate their actions to God, will act without karmic consequences.
>
> 4:24 The liberated let God act through themselves. Whatever they do, it is Brahman that is acting. They always feel at one with Brahman, and that is how they will attain Brahman.

Those who realize that all phenomena are transient and therefore "unreal" *(see 2:16)* will remain composed, do their duty and no longer depend on success or failure.

Wisdom is the highest goal

> 4:33 The sacrifice of devotion to knowledge is more valuable than any other sacrifice. The goal of all action is to acquire the greatest wisdom.
>
> 4:34 Learn by asking those who have achieved liberation. Approach them with respect and humility. They will be glad to teach you their wisdom.
>
> 4:35 You will no longer be confused but recognize all creatures in your Self and regard the Self in oneness with me.

Selfless action is the basis for recognition, and recognition is the gate to the soul's liberation.

Guilt and karma will burn

> 4:36 If you were the greatest sinner, Arjuna, you will still cross the sea of past evil aboard the ship of wisdom.
>
> 4:37 As fire turns all wood into ashes, the fire of recognition will burn all karma.

That is the exhilarating and redeeming message of the Gita: All karma ends as soon as the greatest knowledge is achieved.

Mastering the senses

> 4:39 Those who immerse themselves in the teaching and learn to master their senses will soon achieve recognition. Then they will reach the greatest peace.
>
> 4:40 But the ignorant, who do not trust, who always doubt, are wasting their lives. There is no bliss for the ignorant and the unbelieving, neither in this world nor in the beyond.

The Gita does not define "belief" as blind faith. Belief means recognition through insight into the dimension beyond analytical reason.

> 4:41 Those who have shed all doubt through recognition and are at one with their Self will not be restrained by their actions.

Chapter 5 – Self-denial and the yoga of action

Karma yoga or Sannyasa

At the beginning of this chapter, Arjuna asks the same kind of question as at the beginning of Chapter 3: Is selfless action (karma yoga) or self-denial (Sannyasa) - in the sense of the renunciation of actions - the better way for spiritual development? This subject is often addressed in the Gita. Apparently there were contradictory ideas about this question when the Gita originated.

In 5:2 it is explained that the way of action as well as the way of self-denial (renunciation of energetic works in the world) would lead to liberation. But the yoga of action is called the better way. Shortly after, Krishna explains that only the ignorant differentiate between renouncing actions and selfless deeds.

As mentioned in Chapter 3, in Indian culture, the "abstainer" (Sannyasin) is a seeker who turns away from worldly affairs to achieve liberation and self-fulfillment. He goes into "homelessness", lives off charitable gifts and devotes himself chiefly to spiritual studies and introspection.

It appears that the Gita wanted to reconcile the two contradictory teachings of the time with regard to "selfless action" and "renunciation of action". In the sense of the Gita, it isn't the right way to drop out of society and to renounce all worldly deeds. Much better to selflessly perform the tasks life has burdened us with. In this context, self-denial means renouncing the ego wishes, but acting in harmony with the universal conscience.

Unselfish work is a prerequisite for spiritual development. Unselfish action and recognition depend on each other. Those who serve selflessly detach themselves from the errors of ego. Reversely, selfish action automatically ends when we learn to distinguish the everlasting from the vain, meaningless and transient.

Wise men do not act for their "person", but in harmony with the divine will which is also his own will.

Non-identification

Verses 5.6-9 speak of the requirement to control our thoughts and not to identify with our body. If we observe the processes in our body and our mind, keeping an inner distance, we are on the right way to our Self.

The right recognition and composure as described in Verses 5:15ff. will liberate man from his dependence on the world. He will find the happiness, the joy and the light within himself, and thus the bliss of God (Brahma nirvana).

Renouncing the joys of life?

Some people who are at the beginning of their spiritual training worry that by trying to find composure and inner peace and by renouncing the wishes of their ego, they will forego the joy of life. They fear they must renounce their intensive feelings and their previous great passions.

Yet they can set their minds at rest in this regard. On the right way to self-realization, the soul does not lose its healthy relationship with the outside world. But its relationship with the world changes. "Passions", which were once causing joy and pain, will now turn into true love and devotion in conjunction with quiet, deep feelings of happiness. These feelings cannot be compared with the customary, superficial, brief flashes of ego joys.

Those who walk the way to liberation as described in the Gita and do not engage in pseudo-esoteric aberrations and practices will keep their feet on solid ground. Step by step they will go their way with the greatest spiritual clarity. They do not engage in speculations. They "believe" only what they have realized

Chapter 5 - Self-denial and the yoga of action

deep within themselves. All teachings are only motivation to find their own truth in themselves.

The prudent pupil of wisdom will continue to enjoy transient pleasures, but without depending on them. He will enjoy them while being aware of their transience. In everything he does and experiences, he will remain connected with his inside (Atman). As well as he can, he will always remain in a cheerful, composed state of mind, regardless of what happens on the outside. Thus he will be able to participate in the divine play, the Maya, without anxiety and worries.

> *5:1 Arjuna: You are teaching renunciation of action (Sannyasa), and yet on the other hand you recommend the yoga of action. Tell me which is the better way!*
>
> *5:2 Krishna: Both ways lead to salvation. Yet among the two, the yoga of action is on a higher level.*
>
> *5:3 Only he is truly self-denying who is controlled neither by desire nor by rejection. His spirit, standing above all dualities, is free of the world's commitments.*
>
> *5:4 While the ignorant speak of denials and action as if they were two separate ways, a wise man does not. He who devotes himself to one will reap the fruit of both.*
>
> *5:5 He sees truth, who recognizes that denial and action are one. Both lead to the goal.*

In the above verses, none of the two yoga ways is regarded as preferential. They supplement each other, and both lead to the goal of liberation.

> *5:6 Completeness is difficult to achieve without the yoga of action. However, the wise man who acts selflessly will soon come to Brahman.*
>
> *5:7 Those who are master of their senses, who recognize the divine in all creatures, will not be affected by their actions.*

> *5:8 At one with universal consciousness, they always know: "I am not the one who acts."*
>
> *5:9 When such a man looks, hears, smells, walks, sleeps and breathes, when he speaks or moves, he knows well: It is only nature within the body that deals with the sensory objects.*

Arjuna addresses the problem of "acting or not" in Verse *5:1*, and this becomes relevant once it is realized that it is not the actual man (Atman) who is acting, but that all activities come from the ego, from that which we are not. This ego is governed by the forces of God's lower nature.

Untouched like a lotus leaf

> *5:10 Those who do not adhere to material things and who are connected with their self in their actions, are like the leaf of the lotus, always remaining clean and untouched.*
>
> *5:11 The yogi does his duty without adherence. All his doing serves to cleanse his soul.*
>
> *5:12 Those who do not adhere to the fruits of their labour will have lasting peace. Yet those not connected with the divine will remain slave to their desires.*

Recognition liberates

> *5:15 The Self does not take part in good or evil deeds. Yet this fact is veiled in ignorance. This causes man's confusion.*
>
> *5:16 As the sun makes things glow, so the truth is unveiled when we recognize the Self within us.*

> 5:17 Those who are liberated from all karma through recognition and have chosen the highest as their only goal, will go forth wherefrom no return to earth is necessary.

Serenity and contentment

> 5:19 Those who are rooted in serenity have overcome the dualist up and down of the world. They rest in God who is complete and the same in everything.
>
> 5:20 Those who remain content when they achieve what is welcome and do not become sad when the unwelcome happens, will rest in divine conscioucness.

When we keep our serenity in the face of the welcome and the unwelcome, the soul disregards dualist dependencies. We can see through the play of nature (Maya) and gain independence from external events.

> 5:21 We will no longer depend on external events but enjoy everlasting happiness within us.
>
> 5:22 All joys emerging from material things are also the cause of suffering. They have a beginning and an end. Therefore, Arjuna, you should not adhere to them.

Finding your inner light

> 5:23 He who is not exposed to the power of things and is untouched by desire and anger is a true yogi and will live happily in this world.
>
> 5:24 He will find happiness, joy and the light within himself, thus achieving the bliss of God (Brahma nirvana).

5:27-28 The wise man, who controls his thoughts and his wishes, who harmonizes his breathing, who has detached himself from desire, fear and anger and has concentrated on his inner Self, will be liberated forever.

5:29 It is I (Krishna, the Self) who gladly accepts all denial and all actions with joy. Those who have recognized me as the master of all worlds and the friend of all creatures will achieve eternal peace.

Chapter 6 – Controlling our mind, and meditation (Raja yoga)

All happiness comes from the bottom of the soul

This chapter deals mostly with the taming of the mind. To achieve peace and inner tranquility, we must carefully observe our thoughts and feelings. As long as our mind is dominated by expectations and desires, as long as we are angry and worried, we cannot achieve the bliss of Self.

It is pain to worry about worldly affairs. It is bliss to open to the perfection of the world and to be in unison with it.

Contrary to most people's opinion, happiness is not caused by favourable external circumstances, but when the soul opens to bliss in the depth of our Being.

We should not confuse cause and effect. All beauty is in the eye of the beholder and is then projected onto external things. The things and events we love reflect the love of our divine depth of Being (Atman). Thus all the happiness of this earth does not come from outside things and events but from deep within us.

The creative power of thinking

Just like the universal spirit, so does the individual "spirit" of man have creative power. Everything we think and believe, whether positive or negative, courageous or fearful, creative or destructive, has a mighty tendency to fulfil itself in our life. The "laws" *(Gunas - see Chapter 14)* ensure that our thoughts manifest themselves in the external world. That is how everyone creates "his own world", his body, his environment, his karma. Most people know the theorem, "thoughts are forces", but hardly anyone cares about the associated consequences. If we were aware of the creative power of our thoughts, we would be more careful about what those constantly chattering thoughts in our brain are doing. That way it would be simple to prevent worries, pain and misfortune.

Chapter 6 - Controlling our mind, and meditation (Raja yoga)

Liberation from the compulsion of thought

All our worries and difficulties are caused by uncontrolled thoughts. They originate in thinking patterns implanted in us by parents, teachers, role models, media and others in society. To become free of this automatic, compulsive thinking, we have to learn to observe processes in our mind and thus to become aware of them. Then we can find an opportunity to think, feel and act independently of these established patterns, starting out from our own inner self (Atman) in harmony with the universal consciousness.

It is not a matter of condemning or suppressing our present way of thinking. If we lovingly and most carefully observe our accustomed thinking patterns and the feelings that go with them, they will virtually fade by themselves, and we open up to wisdom and love coming from our heart.

The way to liberation begins when we become careful "spectators" to the games played by the natural forces (Gunas) acting within us. That way, we stop identifying with our body, our thoughts and feelings, our environment and our fate. We are no longer involved in what happens on the outside and in our mind, but we become "pure observers". We desire nothing, we accept everything the way it is. We love the Being the way it is and do what has to be done, whatever the moment expects from us.

If our ego dies that way, our real Self - the Atman we really are - can now light up: the immortal bottom of our soul that cannot be described with words. Then we are one with "Sat, Chit, Ananda" (Being, consciousness and bliss). Those are the words the Ancient Indian scriptures used to paraphrase Brahman, the divinity that is all-encompassing but actually without attribute.

Chapter 6 - Controlling our mind, and meditation (Raja yoga)

Achieving oneness through self-awareness

The review of our inside, the observation of our thoughts and feelings, forms the basis for recognizing ourselves and the world. With such an internal review we recognize the usually crazy hustle and bustle of our ego thinking habits. When we let go of the ego, inner peace becomes possible. Inner peace allows meditation. Meditation connects us with the "oneness". In our mind, the spiral of recognition, contentment, gratefulness, loving service and meditation turns us ever higher and ever more quickly upwards. Thus we can ever more deeply achieve the goal of all goals, the "birth of the deity" within us.

The nature of meditation

Many people who are taking the yoga path think that meditation consists of sitting still and preventing thoughts to come to mind. This is actually more likely to cause struggle and frustration rather than the expected effect.

Meditation is a mental state in which we are at peace and in harmony with the Being. Those who truly meditate take care to maintain this state all day long in the background of their consciousness.

Separate moments in which we switch off sensory perception, as described in Verses *6:11-15*, serve the purpose of practicing concentration and observation of internal mental processes without being distracted by anything outside.

We can only achieve success on this path of meditation if we give up our ego-will and do selfless service. In meditation, restless thoughts connected with our wishes and worries fall silent. Meditation means becoming quiet and thus to create an appropriate space for revealing the Self.

The fate of those who do not achieve fulfillment

At the end of the chapter, Arjuna wonders what fate awaits those who try for fulfillment but do not achieve that goal in their present incarnation. Krishna explains that those who earnestly try, will - thanks to a good karma - in their next life be born into a family where they find ideal conditions for continuing their spiritual path.

Selfless service

> *6:1-2 Those who do their duty without desiring anything for it are called renunciates (Sannyasin). No one reaches the goal who does not renounce his selfish wishes.*
>
> *6:3 To achieve yoga (clarity of the mind), selfless service is necessary. When you have achieved yoga, you can walk the path of meditation, the path of silence and peace.*
>
> *6:4 Only those can achieve perfect yoga who no longer adhere to material things or the fruits of their labour.*

In Verse 6:3, Karma yoga (selfless service) is addressed as the basis for the path of meditation. Only when the soul has been cleansed of the ego wishes, can deep immersion into meditation be successful.

Your mind - your greatest friend and enemy

> *6:5 Man can liberate himself through his divine self. His mind is his greatest friend, but also his greatest enemy.*
>
> *6:6 The mind (the lower self) becomes a friend to those who can control it through their Self. If someone is not in possession of the higher Self, the mind will do what it wants. Thus the forces of his mind will become his biggest enemy.*

Our primary task consists of liberating the soul (Jiva) from egoistical tendencies. Only then will it become possible to be one with our own inner self (Atman).

Chapter 6 - Controlling our mind, and meditation (Raja yoga)

> 6:7 Those who have controlled their lower self and arrived at inner silence, whose lower self (the mind) is perfectly connected with the higher, will remain composed and balanced in cold and heat, joy and sorrow, in honour and dishonour.
>
> 6:8 Those who are master of their senses (their lower Being) and have found their happiness in the recognition of the divine, will have the same regard or disregard for a lump of earth or a stone as for a piece of gold.
>
> 6:9 They have the same regard for all people, whether they are friends or enemies, relatives or strangers, the enlightened or the ignorant.

Yoga of meditation

> 6:10 Those who aspire to yoga (liberation, connection with the highest) should achieve outer and inner silence and in their mind always remain connected with the Self. They will be without expectations, adherence and desire for possessions.
>
> 6:11-15 For practicing meditation, seek out a quiet place and there prepare a comfortable seat. Take your seat. Hold your body, your neck and head erect and immovable. First keep your mind on a point of your body. Observe and control your thoughts and feelings. Finally, fearlessly and cheerfully lift your mind onto your higher Self. That is how you will achieve peace and enter the highest nirvana.

Using simple instructions, the Gita explains how to practice meditation. Several centuries later, Patanjali devised an explicit system of meditation, his famous "Yoga Sutra". Meditation is nothing secretive or special. Mainly it is about wanting nothing, neither holiness nor enlightenment nor anything else. It is enough to be connected with the contented, loving observer within us. All else will happen by itself.

Finding the right measure

> 6:16 Those who eat too much or too little will miss the path of yoga as do those who sleep too much or too little.
>
> 6:17 But those who are modest in eating, sleeping, working and relaxing will be liberated by yoga from all problems and sorrows.

The way of yoga requires not only mental purity, but also the healthiest possible life style.

> 6:18 When the mind is without desires and obsessive thoughts, it can firmly rest in the Self.
>
> 6:19 Quietly and peacefully, like a constant flame in a windless place, a yogi who controls his mind will remain, in connection with the highest Self.
>
> 6:20 Yoga means liberation from thoughts. Deeply immersed, the Self is observed by the Self while the soul feels highest bliss, free from the senses.
>
> 6:21 The soul, which thus experiences the greatest fulfillment beyond sensory perception in itself, always remains founded in spiritual truth.
>
> 6:22 Those who achieve this greatest gain will never deviate from it. Anchored in the Self, they are not even shaken by the worst of suffering.

Chapter 6 - Controlling our mind, and meditation (Raja yoga)

The self in all beings

> 6:29 The yogi sees the self in all beings and every Being in the Self. For him, all Being is permeated by divine love and wisdom.
>
> 6:30 I will not leave those who see me (Krishna) everywhere and who see everything in me, and they will always remain connected with me.
>
> 6:31 The yogi who has recognized the oneness and honours me in all beings, will never lose me from his consciousness.

Control of the spirit

> 6:34 Arjuna: The mind is restless, wavering, stormy and unruly. To control it seems more difficult to me than to catch the wind.
>
> 6:35 Krishna: Without a doubt, the restless spirit is difficult to rein in. Yet those who will not adhere to material things and constantly practice will reach the goal.

Krishna recommends to stop adhering to material things and to constantly practice reining the spirit. This exercise is done best by constantly observing our emotions (thinking, feeling, wanting). That is how man gains distance from them. That is how he is able to see through his ego's obsessive games.

No one who makes an effort will be lost

> 6:37 Arjuna: How do those fare who make an effort in this life to find fulfillment, but who cannot control themselves and do not achieve perfection in their devotion?

> *6:38 Does he perish like a cloud that is torn to shreds by the wind? He does not find the right path and does not find his bearings in this world of phenomena, nor does he achieve oneness with Brahman.*
>
> *6:40-42 Krishna: He does not perish, neither in this world nor in the beyond. No one who makes an effort will perish. After he has reached the heaven of the righteous, he will be born again in the home of good and happy people. Or he comes into the world again in a family with wise and devout parents. However, it is difficult to achieve such a special birth.*
>
> *6:43 In the home of his rebirth he will return to the level of consciousness he had acquired in the last life. Now he can continue to strive on the way to perfection.*

The more he is prepared for self-realization in the present life, the better are his chances for liberation in the next life.

However, spiritual efforts are always like a balancing act between the danger of selfish desires on the one hand and a lack of earnestness on the other.

Chapter 7 – God's lower and higher nature

Many are called, but few are chosen

At the beginning of this chapter, Krishna explains that among thousands of people only a few are striving for divine status. Among those only few reach that goal.

Jesus also taught: "Many are called, but few are chosen." He cited the parable of a wedding feast (marriage with the "kingdom of heaven" - with the Self) to which many were invited. But none of the invited guests was ready to come. Therefore the father of the bridegroom had "good and bad people" come from the street to attend the feast. But there was one who refused to wear festive clothing (to pay his contribution by striving for knowledge and giving up his ego). That is why the host had his servants bind him and throw him into the darkness. He remained caught in his ignorance and had to suffer karmic pain *(see Matthew 2:1-14)*.

Obviously only a minute number of people are ready to follow the invitation of their heart to connect with the Self. There are some who are interested in deeper knowledge of the Self and of the world, but only a tiny number are prepared for the earnestness and devotion necessary to achieve the goal of goals.

The two natures of the deity

In this chapter, the two natures of the deity are examined more closely. One, also called "God's lower nature" (Prakriti), comprises all things and creatures in the universe. God's higher nature (Purusha - identical with Atman or Brahman) is the non-manifest divine being. It is the indescribable, everlasting, all-encompassing oneness reposing in itself.

Verses *7:4 ff.* are among the key passages of the Gita. Verse *7:4* explains that not only did the five elements, *"earth, water, fire, air, space (Akasha)"* come from Prakriti (God's lower nature), but also the mind (thinking, feeling, wanting), reason (Buddhi) and the sense of ego (Ahamkara). These eight basic concepts form the nature of Prakriti. They dominate man's soul as long as he does not fulfil his higher nature (Atman).

Thus, man's soul reflects the two natures of the deity. On the one hand, our body and our mind reveals God's lower nature (Prakriti). On the other hand, hidden deep within our soul, is our higher divine nature called Atman.

The soul is born into the lower nature created by God, namely our body and mind. The higher divine nature, which is present at the depth of everyone's soul, waits for us to make contact with it through our own efforts. That is man's highest goal.

The medieval theologian Meister Eckehart differentiated between two births of man: *"The physical and the spiritual"* or *"one into the world, the other into the deity"*.

Non-identification

The deity reveals itself in the diversity of phenomena. Yet Krishna (Brahman) emphasizes that he does not feel identical with his creations. They are transient, and their reality is therefore only limited and temporary.

Just as God (Brahman) reveals himself in his creations, every human manifests himself in the form of his body and the character of his mind, which he has chosen for his incarnation. He reveals himself in the way he thinks and acts. But just as the deity does not identify with its creations, man should not identify with his manifestations.

The ignorant believe they consist of their body, their mind and their reason. But these belong to the transient manifestations coming from the Prakriti.

Who we really are can best be described as pure consciousness. We are the "stage" on which sensual and mental experiences appear, but we are also spectators to these events.

Chapter 7 - God's lower and higher nature

By identifying with our body and our mind, we limit ourselves. We turn ourselves into transient beings desperately and in vain trying to find support in transient external things.

The "space" in which we can perceive our oneness with the deity (Atman/Brahman) opens only with total non-identification. Paradoxically, what we really are can only become "visible" when we are "nothing".

The Gunas and the Maya

Verse 7:13 addresses the "Gunas" for the first time. They determine the forms and characteristics of all phenomena. They cause the great illusion that accompanies man's sensory perception *(see Chapter 14 for details)*.

In Hinduism, the goddess Maya symbolizes the magic power to create forms. She is the source of the world's wonderful diversity as perceived by man. At the same time, Maya is hiding the divine origin, the perfection and everlasting nature behind the phenomena.

Maya of the phenomena can be compared with a mirage in the desert. Blue sky is reflected in the hot layers of air above the sandy ground. People lost in the desert think they have found water. Only those with the right insight will not be led astray and will not be disappointed.

The world as man usually perceives it has much in common with our dream world. For as long as we dream, we believe that our experiences are real. The illusion leaves us only when we awake. In the same way, "normal" people believe that the world they perceive through their dualist way of thinking represents the truth. Only when they "awake", do they become aware that it was an illusion.

Maya can only be overcome with recognition, devotion and love *(7:28)*.

Chapter 7 - God's lower and higher nature

Man is an actor in the great stage play of Maya. If we don't see through the rules of this play, we suffer from the comings and goings of the dualist events. We may enjoy the pleasant happenings while they last and frown when they end. We may be disappointed when we don't get what we wanted and if the play doesn't keep what it had promised.

Those who see through the play will enjoy it for its own sake, regardless of how it develops on the outside.

The wise man identifies neither with his body, nor with his mind, nor with the roles to which fate may assign him. Just like Krishna, he will be a loving and composed spectator to all that happens. He is observing (compassionately, but not co-suffering) how people are dominated by obsessive ego thoughts and what actions and consequences result.

Focus on God

> *7:1 Krishna: Listen, Arjuna, how you can recognize me without having doubts. Listen to the way of yoga, the way of focussing the mind on me.*
>
> *7:2 I will teach you to become aware of God and man. After this lesson, you will recognize the truth.*
>
> *7:3 Among many thousands of people, hardly anyone is striving for completeness. And even among those who are striving, there is hardly anyone who really recognizes me.*

The lower and higher nature of God

> *7:4 My lower nature, the eight energies that came from me are earth, water, fire, air, space, the mind (thinking, feeling, wanting), reason (Buddhi) and the sense of ego (Ahamkara).*

Chapter 7 - God's lower and higher nature

> 7:5 In addition to my lower nature, recognize my higher nature as well! Be aware of my nature that constitutes the effective force behind all phenomena.
>
> 7:6 Know that I am the beginning and the end of everything that appears in the universe!
>
> 7:7 There is no force above me. Everything in this world is connected to me like a string of pearls.

Krishna the seed of everything

> 7:8 I am the blessing of the water, the light of the sun and the moon, the sacred Om in the hymns of the Vedas. I am the sound of the ether and the special abilities with which man is endowed.
>
> 7:9 I am the fragrance of the earth and the heat of fire, the force of life in all that is living, and I am the denial of the ascetics.
>
> 7:10 You must know, Arjuna, that I am the eternal seed of all living things, the mind of the wise and the glory of the mighty.
>
> 7:11 I am the power of the strong who are without greed and desires.

Here, Krishna describes - as also in Chapter 10 - his most outstanding characteristics in the phenomena of the world. But he also declares himself as the the creator of the three gunas.

> 7:12 The forces of nature, virtue (Sattva), passion (Rajas) and ignorance (Tamas) also come from my energy. They are from me and in me, but I am free of them.

Chapter 7 - God's lower and higher nature

Seeing through the Maya

> *7:13 Deceived by the three manifestations of nature (Gunas: Sattva, Rajas, Tamas), mankind cannot recognize me who is everlasting, standing above all phenomena.*
>
> *7:14 The divine deception (Maya) is difficult to overcome. But those who earnestly practice yoga can see through the Maya.*

The Godseekers

> *7:16 There are four types of man who seek refuge with me: those under pressure, those looking for truth, those guided by the good, and the wise.*
>
> *7:17 Of those, I much prefer the wise. Their devotion is completely directed toward me. They value me above all, as I value them.*
>
> *7:18 All who seek refuge in me are noble men. But the wise have recognized me as the highest goal and dwell in me.*
>
> *7:19 After many lives, those full of wisdom will enter me, recognizing that I am omnipresent. But such souls, Arjuna, are hard to find.*

Again, Krishna expresses that the achievement of wisdom leads to the highest goal, unison with Atman / Brahman.

Man is governed by what he believes

> *7:20 Those who fail to recognize the truth due to their desires, dedicate themselves to the lower gods and practice various rites.*

Chapter 7 - God's lower and higher nature

People's well-being and their thoughts are determined by what they believe.

A creative power is inherent in people's thinking. Those who believe that the world is evil and full of danger are like magnets attracting negative experiences.

Those who worship or devote themselves to low gods or demons (symbols for the egoistical forces in us like lust for power, hedonism, anger or anxieties) will be dominated by them. However, those who recognize the good and perfect in all that happens will earn the kingdom of God.

> *7:21 Whatever someone worships, I let them and see to it that their beliefs will be fulfilled.*
>
> *7:22 Everyone approaches the object of their devotion and will harvest the matching fruits.*
>
> *7:23 Yet transient are the fruits harvested by people of little knowledge and poor reasoning. They will all find the God they deserve. Only those who devote themselves to me will be with me.*

Born in illusion

> *7:24 People of poor reasoning think that I am limited by the forms in which I appear. They do not know my true nature, the everlasting, all-encompassing nature of Being.*
>
> *7:25 Veiled by my creations, I am invisible to the unawakened.*
>
> *7:26 I know the past and the present, and I know what the future will bring. I recognize all creatures, but I am not recognized.*

Chapter 7 - God's lower and higher nature

Man adheres to what his senses can imagine and to his accustomed way of thinking. Usually he sees as reality only what he can perceive with his senses. He is lacking the power of concentration and meditation to advance from the transient manifestations to the "non-manifest" (the transcendent) acting behind them.

> *7:27 People are born in deception. They are blinded by dualist thinking caused by likes and dislikes.*
>
> *7:28 But those who have discarded their ego wishes and liberate themselves from their dualist illusions are able to accept me in their consciousness.*
>
> *7:29 Those who are looking for refuge in me, who strive for liberation from being mortal, will recognize the all-encompassing Brahman, the Self and the workings of karma on which all phenomena are based.*
>
> *7:30 Those who recognize me as the Lord of the universe, the God of gods, will achieve final oneness with me in their hour of death.*

Our dualist point of view is based on our separation from the oneness with all Being. This separation of oneness is caused primarily by our ego will, our likes and dislikes. Therefore it is important to pay close attention to the emotions of our ego, to observe them, to recognize them and thus to liberate ourselves from them.

Chapter 8 – Death and rebirth

At the beginning of this short chapter, several Sanskrit terms are being discussed. For understanding the essence of the Gita, it is not necessary to deal with these. We are therefore reproducing only the most important verses here, with terms such as Brahman, Atman and karma.

Erasing the ego

All beings come from the creative power of the highest deity (Brahman). Brahman forms a centre of consciousness (Atman) in the core of every human being. As discussed above, man's highest task is to connect with this centre and finally to become one with it.

The condition is that we must let go of the mind's obsessive wishes and worries. According to Ancient Indian wisdom, that is how the ego is erased, liberating the soul and enabling it to reach the state of "Nirvana". That is how the soul returns to the oneness from which it separated in the course of its evolution. It thus enters the blissful state of "Samadhi", the conscious connection with the Self.

Jesus compared this process with the return of the "lost son" *(Luke 15:11.32)*. The lost son was "dead" (caught in dualist thinking) and returned to life (to his higher nature, Atman). The brother who stayed home did not undergo this evolution of consciousness (separation from oneness thus enabling the fulfillment of individual divinity).

As the soul reaches Nirvana, it ends the cycle of its rebirths ("Samsara"). Further incarnations are unnecessary because the soul has reached its goal, namely fulfillment of an individual deity in total connection with the universal deity.

The cycles of the universe (Yugas)

Verses *8:17-19* explain how the whole universe is subject to a periodic waxing and waning. Yet beyond that coming and going is an unchanging, all-encompassing Being symbolized by the highest deity, Brahman.

According to Ancient Indian mythology, the universe grows and decays in rhythmic cycles. "Brahma", the creator God, causes the universe to evolve. According to Ancient Indian tradition, each "Day of Brahma" lasts 1000 yugas, the equivalent of many millions of years. There are various accounts about its duration. In any event, the universe "dies", and then an equally long period of "non-manifestation" begins until a new age is created again.

According to tradition, we are presently living in the Kali Yuga (era of the goddess Kali, also called "Black Yuga" or "Yuga of strife"). It is said to have begun in 3102 B.C. In this dark age, mankind is dominated especially by the ego forces such as greed, anger, hatred, fear and worries. That is why this age is especially marked by wars and man's spiritual confusion.

However, this development should not disturb those who are already on the "path of light". It can be understood as an appeal to continue along that path earnestly, courageously, strongly and at the same time cheerfully and with composure.

Do not worry about "black yoga" or "bright yoga". Always keep in mind: "Fate makes no mistakes!" Look after your soul and earnestly sweep in front of your own door. Leave everything else to the wisdom of universal consciousness.

The path of light and the path of darkness

At the end of the chapter, the path of light is described which opens after death to those who have realized Brahman. Those who did not achieve the power to differentiate must continue on the path of darkness.

Brahman, Atman and karma

> 8:1 Arjuna: I want to be able to differentiate better: What is Brahman? What is the self? And what is karma?
>
> 8:2 Also please explain to me how those who have gained control over themselves can become one with you in their hour of death.
>
> 8:3 Krishna: Brahman is the everlasting supreme being, the all-encompassing being. This supreme being forms the Self (Atman), the immortal core of Being in all livings things.

Karma is the power that leads all beings into existence and determines their fate.

The state of Being after death

> 8:5 Those who at the time of their death, when they leave their body, are connected with me through their spirit, will achieve oneness with me. That is beyond doubt.
>
> 8:6 After death, everyone reaches the state that corresponds to the level of consciousness they have achieved in life.

Man becomes what he thinks and believes, that with which his mind was chiefly occupied and connected throughout his life.

> 8:7 That is why, Arjuna, you should fight for inner liberation, always being aware of the supreme. If you direct your thoughts toward me again and again, you will surely reach me.
>
> 8:8 Through constant mental exercises, meditation and turning toward the Self, you will reach the supreme lord (Purushottama).

The supreme Purusha

The Sanskrit word "Purusha" means spirit, man, original soul. In the Gita, the terms Atman and Purusha are approximately synonymous. Purushottama stands for the highest person, the highest being, the deity. It cannot be comprehended with man's dualist mind. God can only be seen in the silence of meditation.

> 8:9 *This supreme being, the master of the universe, is the most subtle that can be imagined; his form is inconceivable. He is pure light, beyond all dualist phenomena. He carries all that is.*
>
> 8:10 *Those who in their hour of death are connected with this supreme being through devotion and inner peace will reach the divine Purusha.*

Non-return

> 8:14 *Those who constantly think of me and do not connect with anything else will easily find their way to me.*
>
> 8:15 *The great souls who have come to me do not return to a new birth. They are no longer exposed to transience and all the suffering that goes with it.*
>
> 8:16 *All beings are subject to rebirth. But those who have become one with me are exempt.*

According to the teachings of Hinduism and Buddhism, man's soul is tied to the wheel of constant rebirth (Samsara). This cycle is seen as sad and painful. One can leave this ominous process by learning to understand the Self and the world, in conjunction with giving up all adherence and desires.

Chapter 8 - Death and rebirth

The day and the night of the Brahma

> 8:17-19 The day of the Brahma consists of a thousand epochs, and his night is just as long. When a day of creation begins, all things and beings in the universe are created from the unrevealed. When the night of the world begins, they disappear again. Thus, the multitude of phenomena is coming and going.

The goal of all goals

> 8:20 Yet beyond this coming and going there is the always invisible eternal Being which does not even perish when all created things disappear.
>
> 8:21 The highest Being is without shape and unchangeable. It is called the goal of all goals. Those who reach it will not return to the material world after death.
>
> 8:22 The supreme lord who determines all Being, the true Self of all creatures, can only be fulfilled through constant devotion.

In practice, "constant devotion" means that man in all his activities always remains aware of the love and completeness of existence. He always ensures to have a cheerful, contented and composed inner disposition.

Two paths beyond the world

> 8:23 There are two paths the soul can walk after death. One leads to a return, the other to liberation.
>
> 8:24 On the path of light, those who have fulfilled Brahman are walking to the absolute.

8:25-26 The souls walking on the path of darkness will return to the world of the senses.

8:27 The yogin who knows both paths will not be confused. Therefore, Arjuna, always remain in awareness of yoga.

8:28 The yogin, who has recognized this, goes beyond doing deserving deeds and beyond sacrifices. He reaches the highest form of existence.

Chapter 9 – The Royal Knowledge (Raja Vidya)

Eternal life

At the beginning of the ninth chapter, Krishna promises the highest knowledge through which freedom of all worries as well as bliss and "eternal life" are reached.

Jesus also repeatedly speaks of "eternal life", such as:

"Truly, truly I say unto you: he who believes in me has everlasting life."(John 6:47)

Understanding the symbolism of the gospels correctly, these words could also be interpreted as follow:

"Those who fulfil God in the Self (Atman) will be eternal in oneness, in the love, wisdom and bliss of the all-encompassing deity".

Therefore, what does eternal life mean? Is the soul not indestructible at any rate, as explained in the second chapter *(2:11-13)*? The Being itself is eternal. As plants come and go in the cycle of the seasons, so does the soul. The constant everlasting element of the soul (Jiva) is its divine core of Being (Atman). But it must first be implemented and lived. Before that, it exists only as an offer, a possibility.

As long as we do not "behold" the Atman (the "kingdom of heaven" within us), the soul is on an intermediate level of consciousness (half animal, half God). That level is characterized by ego thinking.

Only when man has seen through the workings of his ego and has liberated himself from it, can he experience the completeness and unlimited bliss of divine Being. Until then, the soul must go through the joys and sorrows of the world as we are provided with them through dualist thinking.

All is Brahman

In Verse *9:4* we are told, not for the first time, that all life springs from Krishna (Brahman). Brahman, the universal spirit, is the creator, preserver and finally also the destroyer of all beings. Through its lower nature (Prakriti) it makes all things and beings appear while it remains itself untouched by its creations. All phenomena come from God, but God is not identical with his manifestations!

In the same way, man should not identify with the creations produced by his thinking, wanting and working. It is precisely this identification that is the root of all the problems of mankind. As long as man identifies with his body, his dualist thinking, his past, his actions, his strengths and weaknesses, his success and his failures, he cannot accomplish his calling.

Such a soul is born over and over again. It is tied to the wheel of coming and going. Only those who stop all identification with the "not being God" will liberate themselves from the cycle of Samsara and enter a dimension beyond all duality.

The human ego nature

Verses *9:10-13* deal with the ego nature of man. Those who only perceive the material phenomena and do not recognize the spirit acting behind them, pay too much attention to their body and their mind. As long as he does not see through the play of Maya and does not realize his divine nature, he will remain a plaything for the lower forces of nature. He will be tossed back and forth between likes and dislikes, joy and suffering.

Man's consciousness is limited by ignorance. Only when that prison door opens, can the individual soul accomplish its oneness with Brahman, the all-encompassing deity.

Chapter 9 - The Royal Knowledge (Raja Vidya)

I am the way and the life

In Verse 9:1, Krishna explains: "I am the way and the goal". This choice of words may seem familiar to many Christians. Jesus also said: *"I am the way, the truth and the life" (John 14:5).*

This statement applies not only to Krishna or Jesus, but to the divine Self of every human being. If only we can be quiet, stop the constant chatting of the mind, all searching will end, and we are one with the way and the goal.

In that sense, Meister Eckehart explained:

> *"All that God the Father has given his inborn son in human nature, he has also given me. I leave out nothing, neither the oneness nor the holiness. He has given me all that he has given him."*

No one is preferred

Verse 9:29 expresses that no one is preferred by fate. We all have experiences according to our karma and our level of consciousness.

As soon as we connect with our Self, the karma fades, and we are free *(see 4:36).*

> *9:1 Krishna: Because of your trust, Arjuna, I will now reveal to you the all-encompassing mystery. Knowing it will give you freedom and immortality.*
>
> *9:2 This is the greatest knowledge, the deepest secret. It can be recognized through direct spiritual experience. It is everlasting and easy to fulfil.*
>
> *9:3 Those who do not trust my teaching do not reach me and will return to the path of repeated birth (Samsara).*

Chapter 9 - The Royal Knowledge (Raja Vidya)

God is not identical to his creatures

> 9:4 The whole universe is permeated with the mystery of my nature. All beings dwell within me, but I am not limited by them.
>
> 9:5 Although I bring forth and preserve all beings, my spirit is not contained in them.
>
> 9:6 As everywhere in the world, the winds move around in space, and thus do all beings live and move within me.
>
> 9:7 At the end of a world period, all material phenomena return to me. And at the beginning of the next epoch, I create them again in a new fashion (see 8:17-19).
>
> 9:8 All of creation evolves according to my will and remains subject to the laws of my nature (Prakriti).
>
> 9:9 Yet all this action cannot bind me. I always remain the uninvolved spectator.

For humans, this verse is an appeal to be like God, an uninvolved spectator to Maya's play.

Forget all the petty "I" and "my" thinking. Do not adhere to anything. Be aware that everything that comes will also end. Only your consciousness (your divine core of Being) is eternal. Therefore, turn toward this!

Ignorance causes ego thinking

> 9:10 According to my will, my nature brings forth all movable and immovable phenomena. I am the power that causes the world to change constantly.
>
> 9:11 The ignorant do not recognize my highest Being in all things. They only see the material phenomena and therefore do not honour me accordingly.

Chapter 9 - The Royal Knowledge (Raja Vidya)

> *9:12 Determined by egoistical thinking, they are hostile toward other creatures. Yet their knowledge, their actions and expectations must fail.*

Taking part in the nature of the deity

> *9:13 Those, Arjuna, who are not blinded, recognize me as the origin of all and participate in my divine nature.*
>
> *9:14-15 Full of love they worship me and constantly aspire to me. Others follow the path of spiritual recognition. They behold my indivisible nature in all diversity.*

We do not venerate God by externally worshiping him, expecting him to grant our selfish wishes and to end our homespun worries. Venerating God means thinking, acting and being like a god. God rests in himself. He represents the highest consciousness, love, composure and bliss.

> *9:16-17 I am the ritual sacrificial act and the sacrifice; I am the fire, the healing herb, the father of this world and also the mother; I am the object of knowledge, the sacred syllable Om, and the three Vedas: Rik, Sama and Yajur.*

In the Asian religions, the syllable Om is regarded as sacred. It is venerated in chants and mantras. It symbolizes Brahman, soul of the world.

The Rik, Sama and Yajur Vedas are among the most sacred Hindu scriptures.

The inner observer

> *9:18* I am the way and the goal, the lord and preserver of all life. I am the inner observer, the refuge and the best friend. I am the beginning and the end of all phenomena: I am the place of rest and the eternal source of new life.

"Krishna", the "inner observer", is relatively easy for us all to perceive within us. Just try to observe what is happening within you and around you "now". Switch off your thinking as well as you can. Don't think about what you are perceiving now, and don't judge it! Stay in the present! Stay in the state of "pure perception"! If you keep trying this again and again, you will note surprising changes within you.

> *9:19 I am the warmth, I hold back the rain and provide it. I am death and immortality. The Being as well as the Non-Being are within me.*
>
> *9:22 To those who are quite dedicated to me and meditate about me I will give everything they need.*

Those who are connected with the inner God do not have to worry about their external necessities. This is also confirmed by the words of Jesus: *"Seek first the Kingdom of God (the Self within you), and all else (what you need for your life and your happiness) will be added." (Luke 12:31)*

Yet most people do exactly the opposite. They do not pay attention to the God within them, they feel no connection with the inner God, but struggle with their daily worries and problems and wonder why this struggle will not end.

Worshiping other gods

> *9:23 Those who worship other gods and make sacrifices to them do in fact also worship only me, without being aware of it. They are lacking the right kind of knowledge.*
>
> *9:24 For I am the one receiving all the sacrifices. Those who do not recognize me do not receive my peace.*
>
> *9:25 The worship of lower gods and spirits brings less rewards. Whatever men will worship they will be connected with.*

Man puts into practice what he believes. His thinking and believing determines how he sees the world and where his karma will take him. If we see the world as faulty or dangerous, we will suffer deprivation, and we will be threatened by dangers. If we recognize the completeness and wisdom of Being, we will be complete and happy.

Always be connected with divine oneness

> *9:27 Whatever you eat, whatever you do, whatever you experience, do it in the awareness of your oneness with me.*
>
> *9:28 In this way you will be liberated from the consequences of karma following good and bad deeds, and you will be connected with me.*

In everything you do and learn, stay cheerful and composed and be conscious of your divine love and completeness. Forget all wishes and worries about the future and everything that has happened in the past. When you live now and when you are in perfect bliss, you will be in unison with God.

Chapter 9 - The Royal Knowledge (Raja Vidya)

Seeking refuge within the inner God

> *9:29-31 All beings mean the same to me. I reject no one. However, those who turn to me will be one with me.*
>
> *Even someone who is burdened with much guilt will be healed as soon as he seeks refuge with me.*
>
> *Very soon his soul will be cleansed, and he will achieve eternal peace. No one can perish who connects with me.*
>
> *9:34 Always turn your spirit toward me, love me and be devoted to me. That way you will be one with me.*

All guilt and all karma dissolves as soon as we liberate ourselves from identifying with the body and the external events. When we are one with the core of our being, we are one with the universal deity and free of all chains.

Chapter 10 – The power and the glory of God

Krishna the creator of all worlds

In the tenth chapter, Krishna declares himself again as the unborn, beginningless creator of all worlds. He is therefore also the originator of all the characteristics of the human soul, the good as well as the negative.

According to Ancient Indian belief, Krishna is not only seen as an incarnation of Brahman, but also as a manifestation (Avatar) of the god Vishnu (one of the three main gods alongside the all-encompassing Brahman).

To the "knowledgeable" (Jnani), all these legends and deities are only of allegorical importance. They point to the supernatural being that cannot be comprehended with ordinary reasoning.

Only few people are able to approach this realm beyond thoughts and images through meditative immersion. That is why holy scriptures use symbols and allegories to point to the inexpressible and indescribable divinity.

Krishna and his revelations

In this chapter, Krishna describes in what forms he manifests himself in the world. He reveals himself not only as the creator of the beautiful, good and glorious in the world, but also calls himself the originator of fear, disgrace, pain and death.

Man's soul, due to its dualist way of thinking, is confronted with "good" and "evil", "health" and "illness" and many other "pleasant" and "unpleasant" experiences. This way of perceiving the world and of judging it separates the soul from the oneness and completeness of Being. Of course, this separation is only a process in man's consciousness. In fact there is only "one" being that is called God, Allah, Yahweh, Brahman, Buddha or other names.

The meaning of dividing "good" and "evil" and the associated separation of the soul from the oneness is described in Chapter 14.

I am the sun among the heavenly bodies

In Verses *10:21-39*, Krishna explains his most outstanding manifestations. The most beautiful, the most powerful, the greatest and the best are enumerated to demonstrate his glory.

Thus, Krishna is the sun among the heavenly bodies, the Ganges among the rivers, the sacred mountain of Meru among the mountain peaks, the lion king of the animals, and so forth.

All these representations have the purpose of giving the listener or reader of the Gita a picture of the all-encompassing greatness and perfection of the deity acting behind the phenomena.

In these verses, many names - largely from Hindu mythology - are listed. It is not necessary for the understanding of the Gita to explain all these terms and manifestations of Krishna. Therefore they are only presented here in shortened form.

The origin of all phenomena

> *10:2 Neither the gods nor the old sages (Rishis) know my origin, for I am myself the basic source from which they all originated.*
>
> *10:3 Those who recognize me as the unborn beginningless creator of all worlds are free from all deception and saved from all evil.*
>
> *10:4 I am the source of reason and recognition, patience and self-control, inner peace, joy and pain, birth and death, fear and fearlessness.*
>
> *10:5 Violence and non-violence, composure, satisfaction and charity, glory and disgrace, all these characteristics of man have been created out of me.*

Chapter 10 - The power and the glory of God

> *10:6 All the great sages and the forefathers of mankind have been created of my spirit.*
>
> *10:7 Those who recognize my power and the secret of my creative force will be one with me. That is beyond doubt.*

> *10:8 I am the origin of all worlds. All creation originated with me. In that knowledge, those who recognize me worship me.*
>
> *10:9 These sages always have their spirits directed at me. They enlighten each other, and that way they are happy and satisfied.*
>
> *10:10 I grant spiritual insight to those who are constantly devoted to me, and thus they reach me.*
>
> *10:11 Out of compassion I use the light of true knowledge to destroy the darkness of their ignorance.*

Krishna's glory

Chapter 10 continues with Arjuna asking Krishna to tell him more about his glory:

> *10:12 Arjuna: You are the highest Brahman, the greatest refuge, the brightest purity, the eternal divine Purusha, the unborn, all-permeating.*
>
> *10:13-15 All the sages say this, and you demonstrate it yourself. Neither the gods nor the demons know your true nature. You alone know yourself through yourself, O highest Purusha.*
>
> *10:17-18 O Krishna, how can I recognize thee? In what revelations do you appear? Tell me more and in greater detail of your power and your glory!*

Krishna grants his wish and explains:

> 10:19 I will explain to you my divine manifestations, but only the most outstanding, for in fact there are no bounds to all my revelations.
>
> 10:20 Arjuna, I am the Self which dwells in the hearts of all creatures. I am the beginning, the middle and the end of all beings.
>
> 10:21 Among the Vedic gods, I am Vishnu. Among the heavenly bodies, I am the bright sun.
>
> 10:22 Among the holy scriptures, I am the Sama Veda (one of the four Vedic hymns). Among the gods, I am Indra (the highest war god of the Vedic religion); in the living beings I am the conscience.
>
> 10:23-24 I am the fire (Agni) among the fire gods, and I am the Meru among the sacred mountain tops. Among the waters, I am the ocean.
>
> 10:25-28 I am the sacred syllable Om among the words. I am Narada among the Rishis (divine seers); among humans, I am the king. Among procreators, I am the god of love.
>
> 10:30 Among the demons, I am Prahlada; I am the time for all measurements, the lion among the animals and the eagle Garuna among the birds.

According to Indian mythology, demons (Sanskrit: Asuras) are former gods who are devoted to material things. Atypically, Prahlada was a "good" demon and ardently devoted to Vishnu. That is why his father wanted to kill this "wayward son". However, he was saved by Vishnu who appeared as an invincible lion and tore the "evil" father to pieces.

Chapter 10 - The power and the glory of God

> *10:31 Of the aquatic animals, I am the alligator and among the rivers I am the Ganges.*
>
> *10:39 Whatever the seed is among living beings, that I am, Arjuna. Nothing movable or immovable can exist without me.*

At the end of the detailed explanations, Krishna declares:

> *10:40 Endless are my divine revelations. I have only given you a few examples.*
>
> *10:41 You should know that all phenomena expressing the greatest beauty, the greatest power and the greatest glory come from my strength.*

Finally Krishna himself questions the point of giving all these explanations of his power, saying:

> *10:42 But what use are all these explanations to you, Arjuna? Just recognize that the entire universe with all its movements is a single manifestation of myself.*

Chapter 11 – Arjuna's vision

Arjuna "beholds" the highest deity
After Krishna explained his earthly manifestations in the previous chapter, Arjuna now wishes not only to hear in what magnificent form the supreme deity reveals himself, but he wants to behold the indescribable, all-commanding and all-encompassing greatness with his own eyes. However, Arjuna's dualist analytical mind is unable to do so. At his level of consciousness he cannot comprehend the boundless "all" and "nothing" of the deity.

To satisfy Arjuna's curiosity to some extent, Krishna, using his divine magical powers, transforms Arjuna into a special mental state. Arjuna experiences a vision to be understood as a metaphor for gaining some insight into transcendental reality. Arjuna is shown dramatic images depicting the nature of the almighty all-creating and all-destroying deity.

The Apocalypse
The sometimes "hair-raising" images of Arjuna's vision recall accounts of the Apocalypse (prophesy of judgement day and end of the world) as we find them in the myths of Ancient Persia and Asia Minor. The Old and New Testament and especially John's Book of Revelation also depict the Apocalypse in a dramatic way.

However, no judging and punishing God appears in Chapter 11 of the Gita. Main purpose of the story is to demonstrate the mighty, all-encompassing power and glory of the supreme god and to show how this power predetermines and implements all the coming and going in the form of cyclical cosmic events.

All happens according to Gods plan
In the end, Krishna refers to the imminent battle. He explains that the fate of all warriors who participate in this conflict is

Chapter 11 - Arjuna's vision

already predetermined, and that it therefore does not matter whether Arjuna is prepared to take part in the battle.

For the deity, Arjuna is one of the tools to enforce the karma of the participants in the coming battle. Even if Arjuna would refuse to take part in the battle, the outcome would be according to destiny's predetermined plan.

Man with his do's and dont's believes to play an important role in world events. In truth this is an illusion. Man imagines to decide this or that, but in reality it is the universal God who determines and governs.

We should be aware that all external transient happenings on earth are only a play staged by Maya *(see 3:27-30)*.

Your decision

The only important decision man can make of his own during his life on earth and which he must make again and again is related to this question: "Do I continue to adhere to my ego wishes which are connected with the external world, or do I strive for fulfillment of my Atman, my innate divine nature?" In other words: "Do I continue to fight for external happiness, for possessions and recognition, or do I decide to connect with my divine core of Being? Do I remain enmeshed in the transient joys and sufferings of phenomena or do I open up for deep peace, bottomless love and infinite joy within me?"

Krishna's thousand fold forms

Arjuna turns to Krishna with the following question:

> *11:2 You have used elaborate words to explain to me the origin and the end of beings and your infinite perfection.*
>
> *11:3 I recognize the truth in how you have depicted yourself. But now I want to behold your divine form with my own eyes.*

Chapter 11 - Arjuna's vision

> *11:4 If you think I am strong enough to behold it, show me your everlasting Self, O master of yoga!*

Krishna declares himself ready to grant Arjuna's wish.

> *11:5 Krishna: Behold, then, Arjuna, my thousand fold divine forms in the most diverse colours and shapes!*
>
> *11:7-8 Behold the entire universe and what else you wish to see, here united in my nature.*
>
> *But you cannot see me with your human eyes. Therefore I will open a spiritual eye for you. That is how you can behold my transcendental nature.*
>
> *11:9-11 After Krishna has spoken thus, he revealed himself in his supreme divine form, with innumerable mouths and eyes, with many heavenly garments and ornaments, with numerous divine weapons raised, anointed with exquisitely fragrant oils, brilliant and unlimited.*
>
> *11:12 Even if a thousand suns were to rise simultaneously in the sky, their light would not be comparable with the splendour that now burst forth.*
>
> *11:13-14 Now Arjuna saw the entire universe in its infinite diversity, united in the universal form of the Lord. And he was overwhelmed with amazement. His hair was standing on end in shock, he bowed deeply and spoke with folded hands:*

The supreme truth

> *11:15-17 Arjuna: I see in your body all the gods and the host of all living beings. I see the Lord sitting on the lotus flower surrounded by all the sages and all the divine serpents. I recognize your infinite form with innumerable*

> arms, stomachs, faces and eyes. There is no beginning, no middle and no end.
>
> You are wearing a crown, and you are armed with mace and disk. The light that blazes forth from you is immeasurable and difficult to endure.
>
> 11:18-19 You are the supreme truth, the highest goal of knowledge. You are without beginning and without end. You direct everything with your endless power. The sun and the moon are your eyes, and your face is the fire. You ignite the universe with your strength.
>
> 11:20 You are spread out everywhere in the sky, on earth and in the spaces between. All beings tremble when they behold your wonderful yet also terrible form.
>
> 11:25-27 When I see your terrible teeth and terrifying mouths that burn like fire at the end of time, my senses fade, and I am seized with terror.
>
> I see all the warriors assembled here to fight, as they plunge into your terrible mouths to be crushed by sharp teeth.
>
> 11:28 As rivers emptying into the sea so do the heroes ceaselessly empty into your fiery throat. And as moths are attracted to die in flames, these men approach their doom.

The fate of the warriors is predetermined

> 11:31 Arjuna: Tell me who you are who appears in such horrible form! I bow before you and beg for mercy. I wish to recognize you, and yet I cannot comprehend your revelation.
>
> 11:32-34 Krishna: I am the time, the destroyer of worlds. I will destroy the lives of these men because that is

Chapter 11 - Arjuna's vision

> *what their fate is. Even without your doing, Arjuna, all the warriors will have to die in this battle, all but you. So do your duty and kill all those who are already doomed to die through me.*

Seeing and worshiping the deity in all things

Verses 36 to 46 consist of Arjuna's lavish praise of Krishna's abilities. Since these verses contain mostly repetitions and do not add to the understanding of the Gita's message, they are not included here. Krishna's answer is also given in shortened form:

> *11:52-54 As you have seen me, Arjuna, no one else can see me, neither by studying the Vedas nor by asceticism, neither through charity nor through sacrifices. Only those who recognize and worship me in all things can behold me thus.*
>
> *11:55 O Arjuna, be without dependence on and without animosity toward all beings. Take me as the highest goal in all your efforts. That is how you reach me.*

Chapter 12 – Bhakti yoga or the connection with the absolute

Honour God in the absolute or in his creatures?

At the beginning of Chapter 12, Arjuna asked Krishna how we can achieve an awareness of God more easily:

- by selflessly and lovingly serving God as he is incarnate in all beings, or
- by striving to become one with pure consciousness?

Almost the same subject was dealt with in Chapters 3 and 5. Should "Sadhaka" (the spiritual pupil) devote himself to unselfish actions or to "denial"? Should he do good deeds or turn away from the world and find his salvation in meditation?

To be one with the deity (Brahman) means to be God. But how can we imagine God? Is he "all" and therefore also "nothing", i.e. nothing concrete? If God is all-encompassing, can he also be something limited, perceivable with the senses and describable with words? In Verse 12:5, Krishna explains that it is an extremely difficult path to connect with absolute reality beyond words and form, space and time.

God cannot be reached with a dualist mind. All that man imagines about his nature must logically be wrong. You can only open yourself to God by giving up the ego and by quietly being. As the German mystic Angelus Silesius explained:

> *"Naught ever can be known in God.*
> *He is a unique One.*
> *To know Him, Knower must be one with Known. "*

To those who are not yet ready, Krishna recommends the way to honour God through devotion (Bhakti) to his creatures, and through selfless deeds.

Chapter 12 - Bhakti yoga or the connection with the absolute

Serving and enjoying the well-being of all creatures

Krishna answers Arjuna that those who worship God in his creations and work selflessly themselves as well as those who merge with the transcendent Self are fulfilling the Self/Brahman. For both ways it is important, he says, to see through the mental processes (thinking, feeling and wanting) and always to pay attention to the well-being of all creatures.

In Verses *12:2-12*, Krishna describes different ways of oneness with Brahman:

- always feel connected with Atman
- always be aware that the deity is at work behind the phenomena
- control your own thoughts and feelings
- be aware of the oneness and completeness of Being
- serve all creatures and enjoy their well-being
- pause in the stillness of meditation
- do not lust for the fruits of your labour
- strive for knowledge
- end your desires and your attachment

The following verses describe in a very appealing way how to shed ego thinking, thus opening the gate to contentment and true love.

With all these ways, we should be aware that we actually don't have to achieve anything. The "kingdom of heaven" is already within us. We already "are" a divine being (Atman). We only must discard several thousand years of thinking patterns.

> *12:1 Arjuna: Who walks the better yoga way, those who honour you with devoted service or those who try to connect with the unmanifested, everlasting Brahman?*
>
> *12:2 Krishna: Those who always feel connected with me, who perceive me in all phenomena, worship me in earnest faith and serve me - those I regard as complete in yoga.*

Chapter 12 - Bhakti yoga or the connection with the absolute

> *12:3-4 But those will also come to me who open up to the unmanifested, unchangeable, indefinable, to the ever-present, the unthinkable, by controlling their senses, who are composed in all situations and enjoy the well-being of all creatures.*
>
> *12:5 However, those who direct their consciousness toward the non-obvious walk a more difficult path because it requires very deep introspection to approach the unthinkable.*

The way of concentration and meditation was dealt with in Chapter 6 (6:10 ff.).

Always keep your mind on me

> *12:6-7 Those who always think of me in all they do, who wonder about me, who honour me and worship me in devotion, I will soon liberate from the tides of birth and death.*
>
> *12:8 Always keep your mind on me. Open yourself for peace within you. Thus you will be within me, have no doubt!*

One of the most effective and simplest methods of going beyond the ego, beyond dualist likes and dislikes is to keep, in a cheerful and contented frame of mind. That is honouring God. For the god within us is love, trust and bliss.

> *12:9 If you do not succeed, try to practice the yoga of deep inside-oriented immersion.*
>
> *12:10 Yet if you are unable to preform those yoga exercises, honour me through deeds that serve me and mankind. If you think of me in your deeds, you will achieve completeness.*

> 12:11 *If you are unable to always think of me in your deeds, do your labour in a composed manner, without fear and without lusting for its fruit.*
>
> 12:12 *Recognition is better than ritual acts. Meditation is better than knowledge. Giving up all wishing and adhering is better than meditation. With such denial, you can immediately achieve inner peace.*

The truly devoted

The following chapters describe the characteristics of the truly devoted (Bhakti):

> 12:13-14 *Those will be in unison with me who are hostile against no one, but friendly and helpful, who liberate themselves from selfishness, who remain even-tempered in joy and sorrow, always satisfied, going their way toward self-liberation and use their intelligence and their heart in devotion to me.*
>
> 12:15 *I love those who oppress no one and do not let themselves be oppressed, who are without fear and worries and show composure in joy and sorrow.*
>
> 12:16 *I love those who desire nothing, who are pure in their deeds and expect no success, who remain neutral and composed toward everyone.*
>
> 12:17 *I value those who neither adhere to joy nor feel hatred, who neither complain nor desire, who can cope equally with the good and the bad.*
>
> 12:18-19 *Those live in harmony with me who behave equally toward friend and foe, who are untouched by praise and blame, who are silent and always satisfied, who do not adhere to possessions, who are rooted in knowledge and patiently pursue the highest goal.*

Chapter 12 - Bhakti yoga or the connection with the absolute

> *12:20 Above all, I am one with those worshippers who regard me as the highest goal and follow with attention the teaching that is provided here.*

Chapter 13 – The field and the knower of the field

Prakriti and Purusha

In the introductory verse of Chapter *13* (this verse is usually not included when the verses are counted), Arjuna asks about the meaning of the terms "Prakriti" and "Purusha".

Prakriti is called "the field" and Purusha "the knower of the field". In the Ancient Indian doctrine of wisdom, Prakriti is regarded as the original matter from which creation evolved. In the Gita, the term "Prakriti" is used for the phenomena of nature.

The counter pole is "Purusha", the "knower of the field". He is the one who can observe and comprehend the field. In the Gita, the term "Purusha" is used for Atman as well as for Brahman (also "Purushottama" - supreme God).

In Ancient Indian legend, the deity created the world with the help of the laws of nature which also originally came from it *(see 13:26)*. Brahman, the all-encompassing supreme deity, used three forces which shaped the universe. These forces were symbolized by the three gods, Brahma (the creator), Vishnu (the preserver) and Shiva (the destroyer).

Like two golden birds in a tree

Verses *13:21-22* describe how the human soul is in contact with two fundamentally different worlds. On the outside it is connected with nature (Prakriti) - the body and the mind - and deep inside it is connected with Atman, its divine core of Being.

In the Mundaka Upanishad - one of the oldest Hindu scriptures of wisdom - we find the following wonderful comparison:

Chapter 13 - The field and the knower of the field

*Like two golden birds perched on the selfsame tree,
Intimate friends, the ego and the Self dwell in the same body.
The former eats the sweet and sour fruits of the tree of life,
While the other looks on in detachment.
(Source: The Upanishads, translated by Eknath Easwaran)*

It is easily recognized that in the above verse, the bird eating the sweet and sour fruits is our soul (the ego). On the other hand, it is our divine Self that can serenely watch this dualist play, provided that we are ready for it.

The differentiation between the Self and nature

13:1 The natural phenomena, Arjuna, are called the "field". The knower of the field (the Self) is conscious of this field.

13:2 Recognize me (Krishna) as the Self, as the knower of the field. The differentiation between the Self and nature (Prakriti) means pure wisdom.

To grow beyond the dualist manifestations (the pleasant and the unpleasant), we must differentiate between the transient manifestations and the everlasting Self, the core of all beings.

The predominance of Prakriti in the human mind leads to subconscious thinking and acting. The connection with the Self brings light into the consciousness.

13:5 Nature consists of the five main elements (earth, water, fire, air and space), of the five senses, self-esteem and the ability to think (see 7:4).

> 13:6 This is the field where we find desire and rejection, joy and sorrow, intelligence and will.

The characteristics of the knowers

The "Jnani" (knower of the field) is the unconcerned observer of natural phenomena and of the processes in his own mind. He has shed his ego and thus his shackles binding him to the transient manifestations. He shows this through the following characteristics:

> 13:7 Those who are knowers have the following attributes: humility, non-violence, patience, honesty, respect for the spiritual teacher, purity of body and mind, perseverance, self-control.
>
> 13:8 They are even-tempered towards material objects and recognize the evil of birth and death, age, illness and suffering.
>
> 13:9 They do not cling to children, wife (husband) and possessions and remain composed in the face of all pleasant and unpleasant events.
>
> 13:10 Within themselves they are always connected with the Self, they seek quiet places and avoid crowds of people.
>
> 13:11 They are persistent in acquiring spiritual knowledge and strive toward reaching the highest goal (realization of their Self).

In the following verses, Krishna makes another attempt to explain Brahman, the all-encompassing deity.

On the one hand, the sublime is beyond all phenomena, but on the other hand it works in all things of this world.

Chapter 13 - The field and the knower of the field

Brahman, goal of all goals

> *13:12 I now want to teach you what leads to immortality. The only thing essential that must be recognized is the supreme Self (Brahman). It has no beginning and cannot be called either Being or not Being.*
>
> *13.13 Brahman works in all things of nature, in every hand, in every foot. Wherever you look, it dwells in every head, mouth and eye of this universe.*
>
> *13:14 It has no senses itself, yet it can perceive everything. It carries all beings, yet it is without any of the characteristics of nature. Still, it enjoys the characteristics of nature.*
>
> *13:15 It is within and outside all creatures. It moves everything but is itself at rest. It cannot be perceived with the senses. It is far and yet near to everything.*
>
> *13:16 Even undivided it still dwells in all individuals. It is the creator, the preserver and destroyer of all beings.*
>
> *13:17 Dwelling in the heart of all beings, it is the light of all lights, It is the object of recognition, the goal of recognition and recognition itself.*
>
> *13:18 Those who comprehend this and devote themselves to me will be one with me.*

Nature and the Self

> *13:19 God's lower nature (Prakriti) as well as his higher nature, the Self (Purusha) are beyond all comprehension of time.*
>
> *13:20 All phenomena are born from Prakriti. This nature is the cause and effect of all material and mental processes.*

> 13:21 *The soul enjoys the phenomena of nature. Its involvement with these phenomena is the cause of good and bad karma.*

Nature and the Self are not two separate entities but the lower and higher nature of Brahman.

> 13:22 *The observer, the enjoyer and preserver deep within the soul is called the supreme lord (Purusha = Atman).*

Liberation

> 13:23 *Those who see through the interplay between the Self and nature will surely achieve liberation and will not be born again, regardless of his present karmic life situation.*
>
> 13:24 *Some fulfil the Self through meditation, others through relevant knowledge, still others through selfless deeds in the world.*
>
> 13:25 *Some, who have no self-knowledge of their own, will hear the truth from others. By following these teachings, they, too, overcome death.*
>
> 13:26 *All that evolves, whether movable or immovable, is born from the merger of spirit (Self) and nature (non-Self).*

The spirit provides the impulses. The Prakriti fulfils. The deity lets its ideas take form in the external world. Man, too, through the power of his thoughts, causes his environment and his fate.

> 13:27 *Those who become aware that the Lord, who is everlasting, dwells in all beings, have achieved true knowledge.*

> 13:28 *Perceiving the Lord in everything, they do not hurt themselves or others.*

All that happens is a play of nature

> 13:29 *Those who recognize that all that happens is a play of nature (Prakriti) and that their Self remains untouched, are seeing the truth.*
>
> 13:30 *Those reach Brahman who realize that all diversity of manifestations has its roots in oneness.*

Achieving Brahman means being able to be a composed spectator to all the "ups" and "downs" in the appearing world.

> 13:31 *The highest Self is without beginning and without end and without characteristics. It does not act. Even though it dwells in the body, it is not touched by the body.*
>
> 13:32 *As space is not contaminated by things in it, the Self is not touched by the actions of the body in which it dwells.*
>
> 13:33 *As the sun illuminates the whole world, the awareness of the Self illuminates the body and all material phenomena.*

Chapter 14 – The three Gunas: Rajas, Tamas, Sattva

The Gunas, the "stuff" of life

As the Gita shows, the divine natural forces (Gunas) are working in the outer transient manifestations which constantly change. We perceive the result as a wonderful stage play (Maya) characterized by the laws of nature (cause and effect, energy, gravity, centrifugal force, male and female, coming and going, etc.).

The Gunas are the "stuff" from which the world evolves. The Gunas are also called the "mother" of all phenomena. The creative deity (the logos as it is called in the prologue to the Gospel of St. John) lets the world evolve the way we see it, through the forces of the Gunas.

How the three Gunas are shaping the mind

Ancient Indian philosophy describes the three Gunas (forces of nature) as originators of our dualist view of the world:

- Rajas (desire, restlessness)
- Tamas (lethargy, indulgence, darkness) and
- Sattva (kindness and wisdom)

With the help of Sattva (light of recognition) we can see through the negative ego forces (Rajas and Tamas) at work in our soul and disarm them.

We all can perceive these three forces of the soul within us and within other people. The character and behaviour of a person is determined by the individual interaction of these forces.

Rajas predominates in people who are very active, who are feverishly trying to find happiness in external things and in success. People characterized by Tamas are sluggish and prone to indulgence. They have little or no interest in developing their soul or their mind. People with strong Sattva are open to love, beauty and wisdom. Thus they can largely liberate themselves from obsessive ego thinking.

Duality and individuality

The allegory of man's banishment from paradise (Book of Genesis) vividly describes the origin of dualist conscience in the development of mankind. Adam and Eve ate "forbidden fruit" and thus learned to differentiate between "good" and "evil". It means that a period began in human evolution that was characterized by man's dualist view of the world.

In man's consciousness, this dualist thinking caused his separation from oneness. This separation was symbolically described as banishment from paradise. Since then, man's connection with the universal consciousness (with the all-encompassing deity) has been disturbed.

The Old Testament's "forbidden fruits" correspond to the Ancient Indian idea of the three Gunas. They lead to the confusion of man's mind, cause ego thinking and prevent his understanding of the oneness and divinity of Being.

Of course, this separation event in man's consciousness did not take place overnight, but took many thousands of years of evolution. On the one hand, it led man to the dualist ego consciousness with all its problems, and on the other hand it created the condition under which an individual could fulfil his own centre of divine consciousness.

As long as man - just as plants and animals - remains in the original oneness with God, as described through the symbolism of the paradise state, there is no awakening as an independent deity. Man must first enter the duality, the separation from oneness and completeness, to return - on a higher level of consciousness - to "non-duality".

The way of mankind leads from subconscious completeness (in the paradise state) to apparent incompleteness (duality) and at last to conscious completeness (to the deliberate unification with the Self) - *see also Chapter 15.*

Meaning of the earthly life - the ego phase

The main purpose of our earthly life in a body, connected with the way we think and feel, which is determined by the universe, is initially for us to deal with the world as it appears. The soul receives and unfolds its unique individuality that way, connected with the "ego-conscioucness". For that reason, it is also good and necessary that young people go through the classical ego life phases with their wishes, goals and passions and the associated heights and depths.

Man always suffers from some kind of problem or defect because he cannot perceive the completeness and fullness of "reality" (Brahman). In his ignorance he tries in vain to satisfy his thirst for love, wisdom and fulfillment in the external world. At the same time, he is afraid of loss, old age, illness and death.

Longing for oneness

Yet as a rule, about the middle of life and after the first severe blows of fate, men who are ripe for it, hear an increasingly loud inner voice which recognizes that their worldly goals so far cannot be all for which they were born. This initially quiet but in time more and more clearly discernible voice demands fulfillment of the deeper sense of life on earth. It demands liberation from the pressures of the dualist world, the fulfillment of their true nature, inner peace, bottomless love and perfect bliss.

Liberation of the soul

But how does this liberation proceed? The Gita shows us several steps and ways to reach that goal. They all lead to one goal: to abandon dual thinking and the ego behaviour it has caused. These ways, which have developed from Ancient Indian spirituality, are explained in the Gita in a genial fashion. They can be briefly summarized as follows:

- Jnana yoga: The recognition of where, who, how and what we are, and what relationship our individual soul has with God;
- Bhakti yoga: To love God and mankind as they are, and not only to love what we like;
- Karma yoga: Selfless serving;
- Raja yoga: Observation and control of thoughts and feelings.

Such ways can be very helpful up to a certain level of consciousness. But in the last analysis, we should ask ourselves: "Who" needs the "yoga ways"? It is our ego that is searching and wants to achieve something. The depth of our soul needs no path. It walks the "pathless path". If we could let go all dissatisfaction, all wishes and all searching and just "be", we would have achieved our divine nature. Then we could answer the question about our identity as God and like God: "I am who I am" *(Exodus 3:14).*

Brahman and Brahma

> *14:1 Krishna: Now, Arjuna, I want to provide you with the knowledge that has allowed all sages to achieve the highest completeness.*
>
> *14:2 After they found refuge in this knowledge and became one with me, they will not be born again in the future, and they are not afraid of death.*
>
> *14:3 The great Brahma (Prakriti) is a womb for me: In it I place my seed that causes the birth of all beings.*

The "seed" of God is found in all the world's beings. It forms the core of all humans and is called the Self (Atman).

The three Gunas determine nature

> *14:5 The visible nature (Prakriti) is formed by the three original forces (Gunas); wisdom (Sattva), passion (Rajas) and lethargy (Tamas). The immortal soul is closely connected with these Gunas.*
>
> *14:6-8 Sattva is the origin of light and wisdom. However, through adhering it binds to recognition and happiness. Rajas is passion that comes from desiring and adhering. It binds man to his deeds. Tamas comes from ignorance and leads to lethargy and indulgence.*
>
> *14:9 Sattva binds through striving for happiness, Raja through restlessness, Tamas through foolishness causing illusions.*

- Sattva, wisdom and goodness, leads to recognition and liberation.
- Rajas, passion, leads to endless wishes and desires. The consequence is selfish thirst for action.
- Tamas, lethargy and ignorance, causes deception and misconception leading to dullness and insanity.

Identification with the body and the mind

Man is unaware of his divine nature because his soul is attached to his body *(see Chapter 15)*. That is why he identifies with his body and his mind. He regards himself as a separate being detached from the rest of the world. That is the cause of all his problems and hardships.

> *14:10 As a rule, one of the Gunas predominates in us. Goodness beats passion and lethargy, passion predominates when goodness and lethargy fall behind. Lethargy tries to gain the upper hand over goodness and passion.*

14:11 When light flows through all the windows of the body, the light of recognition and wisdom, Sattva achieves a breakthrough.

14:12 When passion predominates, the result is adherence, greed, unrest and restless action.

14:13 Lethargy, ignorance and self-deception are in effect when Tamas takes over the soul.

14:14 If Sattva predominates when the body dissolves, the soul enters the pure worlds of highest knowledge.

14:15 When a body dies in which Rajas prevails, it is born among people again whose thirst for action predominates. Those who die in Tamas, will be born among fools again.

14:16 The fruit of goodness is purity. Rajas leads to suffering, Tamas to lethargy and confusion.

14:18 Those who are fortified in goodness will rise upwards; those in the shackles of passion will remain in the earthly karma cycle: the lethargic will fall into the deepest levels of consciousness.

Merger with the Self through non-identification

14:19 Those will come to me who recognize that all commissions and omissions are determined by the forces of nature (Gunas) and that they are no longer controlled by them.

14:20 If you can rise above the forces of the three Gunas, you will be liberated of all suffering, of birth, old age and death, and you will achieve eternal life.

Reposing - in joy and sorrow

> 14:21 What are the characteristics of those who go beyond their attachment to the three Gunas?
>
> 14:22-25 Those who neither desire nor abhor enlightenment, adherence and deception,
>
> Who remain even-tempered and composed, observe the events and are aware that it is only the Gunas who are acting;
>
> Who are not unsettled by pain and joy, who have the same regard for a stone as for a piece of gold, who repose in pleasure and displeasure, who are untouched by blame and praise, who remain who they are toward friend and foe, those will go beyond the phenomena of nature.
>
> 14:26-27 Those fulfil their Self and are in oneness with immortal Brahman who do their duty in deep communion with me, untouched by the phenomena of nature. They enjoy the complete bliss of Being.

Chapter 15 – Jiva - the soul of man

The World Tree

In the beginning of Chapter 15, we first read of the strange peculiarity of the "World Tree". The Gita calls it the "Ashwatta Tree". As the symbol of the manifest world, its roots (its origin, its true Being) are at top, up in the divine. Its crown with its leaves (the phenomena) points downward.

Many branches of the tree stretch skyward as well as downward. The downward branches symbolize the material world, those pointing upward symbolize the supernatural dimension.

The tree also has many roots hanging down. They express man's adherence to the world's phenomena.

Jiva, the soul of man

Verses *15:7 ff.* form the Gita's central message. They describe the soul (Jiva) of man, its origin and divine destination.

Accordingly, everyone's soul is formed through the merger of Atman with the phenomena of nature.

As a spruce tree allows the growth of countless new trees every year when its seeds are scattered by the wind in all directions, thus the divinity spreads its seed to procreate new gods.

Just as spruce seeds must fall on suitable soil to actually allow a new tree to grow, so for every human being, the "seed of God" is connected with a body created by nature (Prakriti) and a mind (thinking, feeling, wanting) also originating with Prakriti.

In the same manner, man's "soul" (Jiva) is formed. As the Old Testament also explains, it was designed on the basis of "God's own image" *(Genesis 1:27)*. In contrast to plants and animals, the human soul has the freedom and ability to develop itself and to go its own way within the laws of nature and karma.

In the beginning of its development, the soul is in an interim stage. It is neither animal nor god. Like the Ashwatta tree, it has its roots in the divine (Atman) as well as in its compulsive, earthbound nature. In this development phase, the soul is not yet god, but a "god in progress". For the soul to become a "real" god, other things must happen. Under his own power, man must liberate himself of his "lower nature" - manifested in ego thinking and behaviour - and rise to acquire his divine nature.

The deity (Brahman) offers the basis for the individual becoming godlike. But a "new independent god" cannot be a creature and thus depend upon a creator, but must create himself. This act is called self-fulfillment.

Identification with the manifest person

When the universal consciousness (Brahman) manifests itself in the phenomena of the world, our soul reveals itself in our personality. Just as the manifest world is a grandiose divine selection of forms from among infinite universal consciousness possibilities, so our soul appears as a "person" in a body and mind of its choice in an environment of its choice with a unique destiny it has also chosen.

As a "person", the soul plays various roles in the course of a lifetime before it dies again. Out of ignorance, almost all people identify with this "person" who is born, grows up, plays its roles, finally gets old and sick and fades away again.

As a rule, such persons know nothing about their divine, everlasting origin. They feel as isolated individuals and as such fight for their "existence". They are dominated by wishes and anxieties. This mental attitude causes anger, rage, jealousy, hatred, lust, ambition, a tendency to quarrel, stubbornness, intolerance, stress, depression, etc. Of necessity, this turns a "person" into an "ego".

Hiding behind this drama is the wisdom and love of Brahman. The fact that our person is detached from the oneness and entangled in the suffering of the ego is the price we have to pay for acquiring our "Self-consciousness". As mentioned above, we can develop our unique divine nature only if we separate from the oneness with God (the "universal consciousness"). We must first become the "Prodigal Son" *(Luke 15:11-32)* only to return as an independent being to the father's house.

The dualist view of man

The human spirit functions very strangely: It looks into the "oneness" of all life and beholds it as a "multitude". Instead of recognizing the completeness of Being (of the deity), it sees a world split into "good" and "evil". The human mind needs this dualist view to find its way in the world.

To earthbound humans there would be no concept of light if there were no darkness. There would be no "beautiful" without the "ugly". We would have no sense of living without the experience of perishing. At our usual level of consciousness, one cannot exist without the other.

To "normal" people, there is no "pleasant" without the "unpleasant" lurking behind it. Joy and pain are like Siamese twins to them, or like two sides of the same coin. Adhering to what they like, they also have to experience the painful other side of the coin. Gain is always connected with loss as well.

Only when we cut our adherence to likes and dislikes with the "sword of non-adherence", are we liberated from the whims of nature, from "joy and suffering", and experience the constant pleasure and love at the bottom of our Being.

The sword of non-adherence

> *15:1 We are told of the everlasting Ashvatta Tree. Its roots are on top and its branches stretch downward. Its leaves are the hymns of the Vedas.*

The Vedas are the oldest known sacred texts of Hinduism.

> *15:2 The branches of the Tree of Life stretch downward and upward. Their growth springs from the Gunas. The leaves of the tree correspond to material objects. Its roots growing downward tie us to the apparent world.*
>
> *15:3-4 The true shape of this tree cannot be perceived from the viewpoint of incarnate man, neither in its beginning nor in its end.*
>
> *Cut the roots of this tree - entangled with phenomena - with the sword of non-adherence!*
>
> *Then merge with the fundamental basis of Being from which the universe has sprung!*

Overcoming duality

> *15:5 Those who are free of pride and infatuation, who do not adhere to anything and are connected with God; those who overcome the opposites of pleasure and pain, they will reach the home of the highest.*

Krishna recommends letting go, not adhering to anything, and to accept the pleasant and the unpleasant as transient waves on the ocean of Being.

> *15:6 To glow, this place needs neither the sun nor the moon nor the fire, for the highest Purusha glows from within. Those who reach that place will never return to life on earth.*

Birth of the soul

> *15:7 Krishna: A part of my divinity forms the eternal core of every being. From this core is born the human soul*

Chapter 15 - The Jiva - The soul of man

(Jiva) which unfolds its individuality through the five senses and the human mind.

15:8 As the wind carries different fragrances, so the soul carries with it the forces of the senses and the brain when it leaves the body and brings them back when it unites with a body again.

Walk resolutely on the path of yoga

15:9 In the body, the soul - using its senses and the brain - enjoys the material objects.

15:10 The infatuated do not see how the soul is touched by the phenomena and acts according to the Gunas. Yet those who have achieved wisdom will behold it.

15:11 Those who walk resolutely on the path of yoga can recognize the Lord (the Atman) in themselves. Those, however, who do not control their senses and their thinking, do not recognize him.

I am the light of the sun

15:12-14 I am the light of the sun that illuminates the entire world, as well as the brightness of the moon and the glow of every fire.

I determine the energy of the earth and preserve all plants and other beings through my life-giving power.

I am the life fire of all living beings. I determine their breathing in and out and the metabolism in all the cells of their body.

15:15 I live in all hearts. From me comes memory, knowing and forgetting. I am the the originator and author of the sacred scriptures.

Chapter 15 - The Jiva - The soul of man

The highest Self (Purushottama)

15:16 There are two kinds of Beings in this world. The mortal creatures formed by nature (Prakriti) and the everlasting Self (Purusa).

15:17 Yet beyond those two there still is the highest Self (Purushottama), the Lord, in whom all worlds originate and who is preserving them.

15:18-19 I am the highest Self beyond the transient and the everlasting. I am celebrated as the highest Being. Those who recognize and honour me see through all Being.

15:20 I have now provided you, Arjuna, with the highest knowledge. He who internalizes it will have performed the most important task of his earthly Being.

Chapter 16 – Divine and demonic characteristics

"Good" and "evil" persons

The content of Chapter 16 seems like a dark foreign body that has invaded the Gita. While the previous chapters have a bright, happy and uplifting effect on the soul, the emotional and almost fanatical way in which the author is ranting on about the characteristics of demonic people touches us in a strange way.

Verses *1-3* explain the characteristics of persons born into a divine nature. Then, in Verse *4* and *7-23*, the weaknesses of particularly egoistical people and the "hellish" consequences of their behaviour are painted in gloomy colours and in a long-winded fashion.

In a strange kind of black and white portrayal, the two opposites of divine and demonic people are juxtaposed.

Chapters *17* and *18* also show that the handwriting differs from that in the rest of the Gita. Chapter *17* describes how the very diverging faiths and behaviours of people are influenced by the three Gunas. The *18th* Chapter mainly repeats Krishna's statements from the first fifteen chapters. Similar to the 17th Chapter, it describes in detail the thinking and acting of people under the aspect of the Gunas. Then it describes the four castes which played - and still play today - a determining role in Indian society.

Therefore, readers who study the spirit of the Gita in depth are left with the suspicion that the last three chapters *(16 to 18)* were added subsequently by another author for reasons we don't have to discuss here in detail. In any event, these chapters are mainly of secondary importance for today's readers and their understanding of the Gita's essence. For that reason, we only reproduce some selected verses in this and the following two chapters, to provide some insight and an overview.

The struggle against evil

In the ancient sacred Hindu writings, the struggle of the good against the evil forces was often depicted. Krishna himself was given the epithet of "Madhusudana", which means "Killer of the Demon Madhu". Obviously, the struggle against evil forces was of great importance to the author of Chapter 16. He therefore emphasizes in the following verses the dangers threatening those who have turned away from God.

In practical external life as well as in spiritual practice it is found that the "struggle" against "evil" only causes harm. History has proven this in the persecution of the "infidel" or "believers in other faiths". Abhorrent examples of consequences of the "fight against evil" were the medieval methods of inquisition and witch hunts, and in modern days the terrorist acts by radical "servants of God" against people having other views.

On a mental basis, too, the struggle against bad characteristics causes only emotional conflicts, feelings of guilt and inferiority. "Wanting to be better" than we are means struggling against God's lower nature. We can only free ourselves from our ego confusion through loving and deliberate awareness. Awareness heals while struggle intensifies the evil.

The characteristics of those connected with God

> 16:1-3 *Fearlessness, a purified mind, spiritual knowledge, charity, self-control and the study of scriptures; abstinence and honesty, non-violence;*
>
> *patience, composure, non-prejudice, consideration, friendliness, modesty and decisiveness; strength, leniency;*
>
> *being free of desire and anger, envy and vanity; those are the characteristics of people who have made connection with the divine.*

Chapter 16 - Divine and demonic characteristics

Demonic characteristics

16:4 Arrogance, pride, anger, coarseness and ignorance are characteristics of beings of demonic nature.

16:5 Divine characteristics lead to liberation, while demonic ones lead to suffering and bondage.

16:6 There are people with predominantly divine tendencies and those with demonic tendencies. I will now describe the demonic tendencies in detail.

16:7-11 Demonic people have no God. They do not know any spiritual laws. They believe everything that happens is pure coincidence.

Thus they destroy their reason and become a source of evil. They are insatiable in their desires, arrogant and violent.

They think their lust and their pleasure are the only worthwhile goal in life.

Although driven by fear and worrying thoughts, they do not stop their destructive endeavours.

16:12-18 Driven by anger and greed, they are obsessed with accumulating property. They always want to have more and to destroy their enemies.

They imagine being powerful, successful and happy.

Confused in their egoistic thoughts, they plunge down into dark hell.

Conceited and stubborn, they sacrifice boastfully, full of pride and vanity.

These malicious people, devoted to pride and anger, scorn me, who dwells within them and within all other people.

Chapter 16 - Divine and demonic characteristics

16:19-22 Again and again, I fling these evil, cruel and lowest among all people into demonic births.

Led astray from birth to birth, these creatures do not find me, but sink down to the lowest levels of consciousness.

Threefold is the gate to hell: Desire, anger and greed. That is why man should liberate himself from them.

Those who detach themselves from this abyss will achieve salvation of the soul and will merge with the highest.

16:23 Those who disregard the laws listed in the scriptures and live according to their desires will achieve neither success nor happiness nor highest fulfillment.

16:24 Therefore obey the scriptures in all your commissions and omissions! Recognize the wisdom of the scriptures and do your duty in this world accordingly.

Chapter 17 – The Gunas in all spheres of life

The power of faith

At the beginning of Chapter 17, Arjuna asks what effect the behaviour of those has who honour the gods and bring them sacrifices, but otherwise disregard the instructions of the sacred scriptures. Arjuna refers to the last two verses of Chapter 16 in which Krishna recommends the teachings of the sacred scriptures as guidelines for his deeds.

Krishna explains that every person behaves according to his "faith" (Shradda), where "Shradda" means the fundamental attitude to life. Man's faith is determined by the Gunas predominating within him (Sattva, Rajas or Tamas). His faith in turn influences man's emotional life to a high degree.

The Gunas and man's behaviour

In this chapter, Krishna uses further examples to explain what effect the three Gunas -Sattva, Rajas and Tamas - have on man's different spheres of life. They determine not only his faith, but also the food he prefers, the way in which he performs his duties, how he practices abstinence, and how he offers his sacrifices.

The Gunas determine man's thoughts and decisions. These again form his karma. However, the core of the soul (Atman) always remains untouched by their forces. When the Atman is achieved, the soul goes beyond the dualist consciousness, and no further karma occurs.

Om Tat Sat

At the end of the chapter, the words "Om Tat Sat", are discussed, which in Hinduism are a threefold symbol for Brahman. This symbol was and still is today used in ritual practices, and also as mantra. Mantras are "sacred verses" repetitiously recited as suggestive formulas either by speaking, singing or just in thought. Their content is said to have spiritual power.

> *17:1 Arjuna: What is the thinking and acting of men who are full of faith and offer sacrifices but pay no attention to the teachings and instructions of the sacred scriptures?*
>
> *17:2 Krishna: Like all things in nature, the faith of souls is threefold: either kind, passionate or lethargic.*

Man is what his faith is

> *17:3 A man's faith is commensurate with his nature. Reversely, a man's soul is also shaped by the kind of his faith. A man is what his faith is.*
>
> *17:4 Sattvic people honour the gods; Raja people honour demigods or demons (power and wealth), Tamas-oriented people honour ghosts and spectres.*
>
> *17:7 Faith manifests itself in everything: in the food that is preferred, in sacrifices, in work, in askesis and in the way in which gifts are given.*

> *17:8 Food that promotes health, vitality, joy and contentment, which is sweet, mild and flavourful is assigned to the "goodness" category (Sattva).*
>
> *17:9 Food that is too bitter, too sour, too salty, too hot or too spicy is assigned to passion (Raja).*
>
> *17:10 Food that is unclean, tasteless, foul or stale is assigned to the characteristics of ignorance and lethargy.*

Chapter 17 - The Gunas in all spheres of life

> 17:11-13 Sattva-like is the sacrifice that is offered without thinking of a reward. Raja-like is the sacrifice that is offered expecting personal reward or recognition. A sacrifice is Tamas-like when it is offered without any associated faith.

Types of askesis

> 17:14 Askesis of the body consists of honouring the deity, the spiritual guide, wise men, and cleanliness, honesty, abstinence and non-violence.
>
> 17:15 Askesis in speech is when it is truthful, friendly and useful.
>
> 17:16 Askesis of the mind is marked by quiet cheerfulness, friendliness, silence, self-control and purity.
>
> 17:17-19 Askesis is Sattvic when it is executed in the right faith, without requiring a reward and harmonically; it is Raja-like when it is done to achieve honour and adoration; it is Tamas-like when it is connected with confused ideas or self-torture.

> 17:20-22 Charitable gifts according to Sattva is not connected with expecting gifts in return. They are given at the right time and at the right place to those who really need help.
>
> Raja-like charitable gifts are given unwillingly or in consideration of personal recognition or advantages; they are Tamas-like when they are given in the wrong place, at the wrong time, to an unworthy person or without respect for the recipient's person.

17:23-26 "Om Tat Sat" - these words symbolize Brahman in a threefold manner.

That is why sacrificial practices, charity and ascetic acts are initiated by speaking the word "Om".

We say "Tat" when we perform sacrifices, give to charity and practice askesis without asking for a reward.

The word "Sat" means the "Good" and the "Being". That is why it is used with laudable deeds.

Chapter 18 – Denial and liberation

Action or non-action

The *18th* Chapter can be understood as a summary and repetition of all other chapters.

In the beginning of the chapter, the subject of "action" or "refraining from all actions if possible" is dealt with again.

Krishna explains that it is important to offer sacrifices and give to charity as well as to practice abstinence. However, actions should by no means be performed with rewards in mind. It would also be wrong to deny doing one's duty.

Verses *20 ff.*, with reference to the Gunas, describe the three kinds of knowledge. They also explain how people act who are marked by Sattva, Raja or Tamas. In the end, three kinds of joys are explained with reference to the Gunas.

None of these verses contain anything particularly new.

The difference between castes

Starting at Verse *40* is an explanation of the caste system in the Ancient Indian tradition, which still applies today. In society, the Brahmins (priests) hold the highest rank. They are followed by the Kshatriyas (rulers and warriors). Next in the hierarchy are the Vaishyas (farmers, merchants and artists). The fourth and last caste is formed by the Shudras (tradesmen, servants, labourers). The Gita does not mention the "untouchables" who are outside the four castes.

In this chapter, it is pointed out how important it is to perform the work appropriate to one's own caste. It is better to perform one's own tasks imperfectly than to complete work belonging to another caste.

Verses *49 ff.* explain how we can achieve the fulfillment of Atman or Brahman. These verses tell us nothing that wasn't already discussed in the previous chapters.

In the end, Krishna emphasizes that his teachings should never be passed on to the unworthy who do not practice askesis and do not honour God.

Conditions for becoming one with Brahman

> *18:5 Krishna: You should not renounce the actions of sacrifice, charity and askesis, for these will purify you.*
>
> *18:10 The wise man who practices denial and has stopped doubting, whose mind is endowed with goodness (Sattva), is not averse to unpleasant acts and is not attached to agreeable acts.*

Recognition, acting, reason and perseverance

> *18:20 Sattva-like is the recognition in which you see the everlasting Being in all creatures as an indivisible whole.*
>
> *18:26 Those are regarded as marked by Sattva who act without bondage, resolutely and energetically, unmoved by success or failure.*
>
> *18:30 It is Sattva-like reason if a man knows what to do or not to do, recognizing what keeps man's mind in bondage and what liberates him.*
>
> *18:35 It is Tamas-like for a man to show the kind of persistence that does not abandon ignorance, laziness, fear, grieving, depression or arrogance.*

Sattva joy

> *18:36-37 That joy is regarded as Sattva-like in which you achieve true happiness and contentment through perseverance and carefulness. It leads to the end of all suffering. Such joy tastes like poison in the beginning and like nectar in the end.*
>
> *18:38 That joy is Rajas-like which springs from contact with material things. It tastes like nectar in the beginning and like poison in the end.*
>
> *18:39 That joy is Tamas-like which comes from lethargy or ignorance.*

Perform the tasks that fit your own nature

> *18:40 The tasks of all beings are determined by the three Gunas. Brahmins, Kshatriyas, Vaishyas and Shudras differ in the nature that has been assigned to them.*
>
> *18:42 The actions of Brahmins are marked by cheerfulness, self-control, inner peace, modesty, wisdom, leniency and patience.*
>
> *18:43 Characteristics of the Kshatriyas are heroism, strength, determination and generosity.*
>
> *18:44 Work that suits the nature of Vaishyas consists of growing crops and raising cattle, engaging in trade and commerce. The duties of Shudras are to serve the others.*
>
> *18:45 Those reach completeness who do their duty according to their calling and who in their work honour that from which all beings spring.*
>
> *18:47 It is better to do your own work imperfectly than to perform those duties perfectly which are assigned to others. Those who perform the duties to which they were born do not incur karma.*

Chapter 18 - Denial and liberation

Achieving oneness with Brahman

18:50 Krishna: Now hear, O Arjuna, this supreme knowledge: How those who have achieved completeness will become one with Brahman;

18:51-53 Those will be one with Brahman who purify their thinking, no longer adhere to material objects, are not moved by likes or dislikes, who live in seclusion and abstinence;

who control their speech, their body and their mind, always connected with their innermost Being through meditation;

who have abandoned egoism, violence, pride, desire, anger and the need to own property;

who are quiet of spirit, always cheerful and composed.

18:54 Those who are thus rooted in the absolute will never complain or desire anything. They are even-tempered toward all beings. That is how they will achieve the highest state of devotion to me.

18:55 Through such devotion they will recognize my true Being. With that awareness they will become one with me.

18:58 If you are always one with me, my strength will help you to surmount all difficulties. However, those who refuse to hear my words out of egoism will perish.

The Lord directs all movements

18:61 The Lord resides in the hearts of all people, directing their movements. Through the power of Maya, he moves them as if they were driven by a machine.

18:62 Turn to the Lord, O Arjuna, with all your heart! Through his grace, you will achieve supreme peace and eternal life.

Chapter 18 - Denial and liberation

Give up all religions

> *18:63 Now I have provided you with the most secret knowledge. Think about it thoroughly! Then you can do what you feel is right, and you will make no mistakes.*
>
> *18:66 Give up all ideas of dharma (duty, religion, virtue, law) and seek refuge only in me. I will deliver you from sin and all evil. Do not despair!*

If we want to interpret this last verse positively, we could say: Not commandments or prohibitions should determine our thinking and acting, but the voice of the pure heart.

If we have internalized the "essence of the Gita", we should not stand still, neither with this "sacred scripture" nor any other, neither with the Hindu religion nor any other, but continue from here. As Gautama Buddha says in the Diamond Sutra, all teachings are only vehicles and should not be venerated as eternal wisdom.

> *"Bhikkus, you must know that all the teachings I give you are a raft. In the end, all teachings, to say nothing of the non-teachings, must be given up."*

Conclusion – The essence of the Gita

The deity within you

The essence of the Gita can be summarized as follows:

- All is one, all is God. All springs from the deity and all is carried by it.
- If all is God, then all people must be God as well. Become aware of the divinity within you and live accordingly!
- If all is God, I can trust that all will be best and that fate makes no mistakes. Therefore, no one has to worry, and no anxiety is justified.
- You are not identical with your body and your mind. You are the god within you (Atman), and that god does not differ from the universal deity (Brahman).
- Everything created is ephemeral. Everything has a beginning and an end. However, the Self within us is not created. It is like Brahman without beginning and without end. It exists independently of time and space.
- The individual deity is installed within us. If the soul merges with it, it meets the purpose of its earthly life.
- We do not liberate ourselves if we flee from the requirements of fate and escape from external life. But by doing what the game of life demands of us "now", and if we are constantly aware of the divinity and completeness of every moment.

The Gita gives us many excellent suggestions on how to recognize and fulfil ourselves. Yet all such efforts will have limited success for as long as we stay mentally separated from God.

Therefore we cannot grasp the essence of the Gita if we only identify with the "pupil" (Arjuna) and fail to recognize that we are also the "teacher" (Krishna) and are therefore called upon to reveal supreme wisdom and love.

Conclusion - The essence of the Gita

Acting in all men are Arjuna and Krishna, the earthbound more or less ignorant soul (Jiva) and the divine boundless depth of our soul (Atman).

Thanks to the creative force of our imagination and thoughts, everyone can decide with what to identify. We are what we think we are. We feel the way we judge ourselves. If we identify with our body and the usual thinking patterns, we will perceive ourselves as small, abandoned, always in danger, transient and separated from the divine glory and fullness of life. If we live without such limits, we open toward love within the depth of our soul, toward the love from which it all came, we trust in the divinity and completeness of Being and achieve our kingdom.

Blasphemy

In the eyes of Christian "Pharisees", it is blasphemy when a man claims divinity for himself. Even Jesus was persecuted by the Jews, and they wanted to stone him because he declared: *"I and the Father are one" (John 10:30).* He defended himself, pointing to *Psalm 82:6*, which says about men: *"You are gods; you are all children of the Most High".*

Twelve hundred years later, inquisition proceedings were opened against Meister Eckehart because he called the depth of the soul divine and declared: *"All that is within God's nature is also within the just and godly man; that is why such a man also works the way God works ..."*

With that conviction, Eckehart also did not differentiate between Jesus and himself. He declared that *"All that God the Father gave his only begotten son in human form, He also gave me: I leave out nothing, neither the union nor the holiness, He gave me everything the way he gave it to him."*

Just like Eckehart, everyone can be confident not only to have been created in the image of God, but to be able anytime to achieve "his oneness with the Father".

Conclusion - The essence of the Gita

Ego and being God

Of course there is the danger that a man's ego becomes immoderately bloated when he relates the message of "being God" to himself. Such an ego confuses "being God" with exercising power, with vanity, with being "better" and "wanting to be holy".

Such a man would shed his ego by recognizing that "being God" means loving and serving. The ego would be liberated if the man would understand how pointless, ridiculous and unjustified worries and anxieties, anger, envy, expectations and desires are for a divinity.

Ego awareness includes splitting the world into "good" and "evil". With their dualist thinking, people cannot imagine that all Being is complete and safe within the deity. They cannot imagine that with God "every hair is numbered". *(Luke 12:7)* Their eyes are preferably on the evil, the dangerous, the sad and the cruel of the world. Their ego sees only the ephemeral and evaluates it in its common way. It recognizes no sense behind its suffering.

Wise men live beyond dualist evaluation

As the Gita explains, those with understanding remain composed and unmoved about worldly pleasures and suffering, joy and pain. They know that they are coming and going. They are aware that these experiences refer only to the body and the mind. Smiling and always in harmony with themselves, they observe the Maya, the divine play of phenomena.

They are liberated from the pressure of thinking patterns. They realize that looking down from a higher level, everything is well the way it is. They know: "Fate makes no mistakes!" Their awareness has gone beyond dualist thinking and judging.

The imperfection of the dualist world

Again and again, people on the spiritual way to awakening pose this question: Why is there so much pain and suffering in the world if allegedly everything is permeated and carried by the deity?

The counter question is: What man would move even a millimetre away from the paradise of his comfort zone and strive for the fulfillment of his being God if it weren't for pain, caused by his dualist way of thinking, that is pulling him away from behind his cosy warm stove? He would be bogged down in the swamp of "Tamas" if he were continuously living in the land flowing with milk and honey.

Only through recognizing and by shedding our ego is it possible for us to pass over from an animal/human consciousness to a divine.

"Normal" people are so busy with the ups and downs of the waves on the ocean surface that they cannot fathom the blissful endless expanse and depth of the sea. So tightly are they under the spell of transient joys and sorrows in the dualist world that they do not become aware of the "kingdom of heaven" at the depth of their soul.

Only when they see through the play of the waves, the play of the Maya staged by the deity, will they achieve liberation form all evil and be connected with the bliss of Atman and Brahman.

Breaking through things

The Gita is not fond of people looking for salvation by retreating from the world. Instead it encourages us to energetically and selflessly perform the work that fate has in store for us.

Conclusion - The essence of the Gita

In that sense, Meister Eckehart also declared:

"Man should not flee from things and go into solitude, but he must learn to break through things and to take hold of his God within."

Not the "what" we do is essential, but the "how", meaning the inner attitude with which we act. Therefore we should always take care that we do our daily work with a cheerful, composed and loving frame of mind.

In that way we are connected with the depth of our soul, and we are able to take hold of "God within".

Index

A

Ahamkara 67, 69
Akasha 66
Ananda 59
Angelus Silesius 98
Arjuna 16
Asanas 34
Ashwatta Tree 116
Asuras 91
Atman 14, 17, 29, 76, 80, 136
Avatar 16, 45, 88

B

Bhagavad 10
Bhakti 34, 98, 101, 112
Bharata 21
Bhikkus 134
Blasphemy 136
Brahma 75, 78, 103, 112
Brahman 17, 67, 76, 81, 98, 99, 106, 112
Brahma nirvana 33, 53, 56
Brahmins 130, 132
Buddhi 44, 67, 69

C

Castes 130
Chit 59

D

Demon 72, 123
Demonic 124
Devaki 17
Dharma 16, 48, 134
Diamond Sutra 134
Duality 31, 110, 119
Duryodhana 21

E

Ego 32, 74, 81, 83, 111
Eternal life 80

G

Gautama Buddha 35, 134
Gita 10
Gunas 36, 68, 71, 109, 113, 126

H

Hatha yoga 34
Homelessness 35, 52

I

Ikshvaku 45, 47
Indra 91

J

Janaka 42
Jesus 17
Jiva 61, 80, 116, 120, 136
Jnana 34, 40, 45, 112
Jnani 88, 105

K

Kali Yuga 75
Karma 34, 36, 40, 43, 47, 51, 52, 76, 82, 112
Kauravas 21, 22
Kingdom of God 18, 85
Kingdom of heaven 18, 39, 80, 138
Krishna 16, 17
Kshatriyas 130, 132
Kuru battlefield 16
Kurukshetra 21

L

Lost son 74

M

Madhusudana 123
Mahabharata 16, 19
Mahatma Gandhi 31
Manas 44
Maya 68, 71, 137
Meditation 58, 62, 76, 101
Meister Eckehart 67, 82, 136, 139
Meru 89
Middle Way 35
Mind 26
Mundaka Upanishad 103

N

Nirvana 74

O

Om 70, 84
Om Tat Sat 126

P

Pandavas 21
Patanjali 62
Prahlada 91
Prakriti 36, 66, 81, 83, 103, 106, 108
Pranayamas 34
Purusha 66, 77, 90, 103, 106
Purushottama 76, 103, 121

R

Raja 34, 58, 112
Rajas 70, 109, 113
Raja Vidya 80
Ramana Maharshi 46
Rebirth 65, 77
Reincarnation 25
Rishis 13, 14

S

Sadhaka 98
Samkhya 15
Samsara 25, 74, 77, 81
Sannyasa 35, 46, 52, 54
Sannyasin 52, 61
Sat 59
Sattva 70, 109, 113
Self 29, 76, 104, 107, 115
Shiva 103
Shradda 126
Shudras 130, 132

T

Tamas 70, 109, 113

U

Untouchables 130
Upanishads 15

V

Vaishyas 130, 132
Vedas 15, 84
Vishnu 17, 20, 88, 91, 103
Vivasvat 45, 47
Vyasa 20

W

World Tree 116

Y

Yoga 34, 40, 45, 52, 58, 62, 98, 112
Yoga Sutra 62
Yugas 75

Recommended books

"The crown jewel of Shankara"

Newly mounted by
Bernd Helge Fritsch

Adi Shankara (788-820 A.D.) is regarded as the most important Indian spiritual philosopher and reformer of Hinduism. His famous major work was "Viveka Chudamani" (Jewel of Distinction). It is considered the "crown jewel" of ancient Indian wisdom. The present edition offers the reader a modern translation of the "jewel" and a careful selection from the originally 580 Sanskrit verses. The author has left out numerous repetitive passages as well as statements not in keeping with our modern *zeitgeist*.

Bernd Helge Fritsch, himself a spiritual teacher, has added explanations to many verses, to clarify the meaning of Shankara's text which is now approximately 1200 years old.

This book deals with the central questions of our life: What constitutes the meaning of my life? How do we explain our destiny? How do we liberate ourselves from worries, illness and suffering? How can we connect ourselves with the everlasting beauty, love and bliss at the fundamental basis of Being?

Buchempfehlung

"Der große Prinz und das Glück"

Bernd Helge Fritsch

Rund 80 Jahre nachdem Antoine de Saint-Exupéry, Schriftsteller und Flugpilot, dem "Kleinen Prinz" in einer afrikanischen Wüste begegnen durfte, erscheint wieder ein "Prinz" von einem andern Stern auf unserer Erde. Es ist der "Große Prinz", der hier auf unserem Planeten das Leben und das Glück der Menschen studiert.

In diesem Buch wurden seine Erfahrungen und Erkenntnisse über das "Glücklich-Sein" niedergeschrieben.

Ein Buch, das uns das "WunderLeben" mit neuen Augen betrachten lässt.

Ein Buch, das uns dem Geheimnis eines *"tiefen und anhaltenden Glücklich-Seins"* näher bringt.

Buchempfehlung

Vom Umgang mit der Zeit
99 spirituelle Anregungen

Bernd H. Fritsch

In diesem Hand-Buch findest du 99 Aphorismen für ein "Leben in der Zeit und in der Zeitlosigkeit".

Alle wesentlichen Lebensbereiche des Menschen, wie beispielsweise: Liebe, Freundschaft, Gesundheit, Freude, Umgang mit Konflikten, Beendigung von Schuldgefühlen, Fehler machen dürfen... werden in diesen Aphorismen in prägnanter und gut verständlicher Weise angesprochen. Ein idealer Begleiter um sich zu besinnen, um auf deinem Weg das Wesentliche vom Unwesentlichen zu unterscheiden.

Du findest in diesem Brevier leicht lesbare Anregungen zu einem Leben in Frieden und Vollkommenheit, frei von Zeitdruck, Stress, Ängsten und Sorgen.

Aufgezeigt wird, wie durch die Erkenntnis des Sinns unseres Daseins und durch die richtige Einstellung zu unseren Aufgaben, jeder Augenblick unseres Erdenleben etwas Besonderes sein kann.

Der Autor hat in diesem kleinen Büchlein all seine, im Laufe von rund sieben Jahrzehnten gewonnenen Erkenntnisse, zusammengefasst. Für den, der bereit ist sich auf die Weisheiten in dieser Schrift einzulassen, werden sich neue Dimensionen eröffnen.

Buchempfehlung

WU-WEI
erfolgreich Nichts tun

Bernd Helge Fritsch

Dieses Buch beinhaltet eine Auswahl von Essay-Briefen, wie sie von Bernd Helge Fritsch seit etlichen Jahren in Mail-Form an Freunde und Interessierte versendet werden. Diese Briefe behandeln die wichtigsten Lebensfragen. Zu diesen zähle ich:

- Was ist der Sinn unseres Erdendaseins?
- Wer bin ich?
- Wie lebt man erfüllende Beziehungen?
- Vom Umgang mit Depressionen
- Wie kann ich glücklich sein, unabhängig von äußeren Ereignissen?
- Was geschieht mit mir nach meinem körperlichen Tod?

Diese Essay-Briefe sollen keine "Glaubensinhalte" vermitteln. Der Autor möchte kein "gläubiger Mensch" sein und gehört deshalb auch keiner Religionsgemeinschaft an. Wohl aber ist nach seiner Ansicht "Religion" (die bewusste Verbindung mit dem Höchsten) unsere wichtigste Mission auf dieser Erde.

Please write to us!

Please write to us!

Please write to us if you……

- ….want to ask the author, Bernd Helge Fritsch, any questions;

- ….are prepared to give us suggestions and feedback;

- ….want to have information about lectures and seminars by Bernd Helge Fritsch;

- ….want to receive our free monthly "Essay Letter" by email.

We welcome every letter or message and will be happy to reply.

Email: office@berndhelgefritsch.com

Visit our homepage:
www.berndhelgefritsch.com